VORTEX 01
BELMONT BRIDGE

WITH EDUARDO ARROYO | NO.MAD
ARTICLES BY: INAKI ALDAY | EDUARDO ARROYO | ROBIN DRIPPS

UNIVERSITY OF VIRGINIA SCHOOL OF ARCHITECTURE

Co-Sponsor
University of Virginia Arts Council

Articles
Iñaki Alday, Quesada Professor and Chair, Department of Architecture
Eduardo Arroyo, Jaquelin T. Robertson Visiting Professor
Robin Dripps, David Fitzgibbon Professor Of Architecture

Editor
Iñaki Alday, Quesada Professor and Chair, Department of Architecture

Editorial Team
Nathan Burguess MLA '13
Rebecca Hora MArch '13
Katherine Treppendahl MArch '12
Alex Ayala MArch '14

Editorial Council
Ghazal Abbasy-Asbagh, Lecturer
Rebecca Cooper, Fine Arts Architecture and Instruction Librarian
Robin Dripps, T. David Fitzgibbon Professor of Architecture
Charles Sparkman, Lecturer

Spring 2013
Dani Alexander, MLA '14
Rebecca Hora, MArch '13
Carlos Jennings, BSA '13
Matthew Pinyan, MArch '13
Ryan Metcalf, MArch '13

Fall 2012
Pheobe Harris, BSA '14
Rebecca Hora, MArch '13
Nick Knodt, MArch '14
Matthew Pinyan, MArch '13
Mariam Ramahtullah, BSA '14
Kate Stabler, BSA '14
Clayton Williams, MArch '14

Spring 2012
Nathan Burgess, MLA '13
Brian Davis, MArch '12
Nicole Keroak, MArch '12
Charles Sparkman, MArch '12
Katherine Treppendahl, MArch '12

CONTENTS

PROCESS

ESSENTIAL COMPLEXITY // COMPLEJIDAD ESENCIAL
    EDUARDO ARROYO

WINNING PROPOSALS
    ARROYO AWARD
    PUBLIC AWARD
    FACULTY AWARD
    STUDENT AWARD

OBSERVATIONS ON A BRIDGE
    ROBIN DRIPPS

TEAM PROPOSALS

MUDDY HANDS
    IÑAKI ALDAY

PROCESS

This is the result of an innovative pedagogical and experimental workshop for 10 days engaging almost the whole School of Architecture of the University of Virginia. It has been a unique experience in the collaboration between the city, the community and the school, an incredibly powerful potential resource for Charlottesville. The departments of Architecture and Landscape Architecture have been fully involved with 319 students organized in 29 teams with one or more faculty in each of them as advisors. Other departments, Architectural History and Urban and Environmental Planning, also joined the experiment. All teams benefited from the overall leadership of one of the most outstanding Spanish architects, Eduardo Arroyo. The Belmont Bridge is obviously crossing over the rail tracks and connecting Belmont and downtown, as well as being part of a larger network. And it has to be efficient for motor vehicles in local traffic and larger scale traffic, as well as being comfortable, safe and pleasant for pedestrian and bicycles. But a bridge, or let's say just a crossing, can be much more than a complex traffic infrastructure, especially in such an interesting and delicate context. A bridge is also a place to look from and to look at, a place to stay and enjoy. One cannot understand some of the most beautiful cities in the world without enjoying its bridges: Venice, Paris, Prague, Amsterdam… Bridges are buildings itself that can be used for more purposes (Ponte Vecchio in Florence, Rialto in Venice but also recent ones as the bridge-pavilion of Zaha Hadid in Zaragoza) and should be always a public space. The Belmont Bridge is the welcoming gateway to Belmont and to the Downtown Mall, the most important pedestrian transformation in the United States at that time, designed by Lawrence Halprin in the mid '70s. And the renewal of the bridge is an enormous opportunity for rethinking this link, the end of the mall and what happens to the East, the potential of the vacant spaces to the south of the rail tracks and perhaps to spread and expand the powerful civic space of the mall further away, increasing the density and the urban condition. Infrastructures are, today, proved to be the key places of opportunity in the European and American cities of all sizes. And nowadays, tracks, bridges, coverings and all related to the technological changes in railroad transportation, are allowing to developing new concepts in architecture and public space. The workshop has also been a way to participate in the Belmont Bridge Gait-way competition, organized by members of the local community leaded by Brian Wimer. The outcome of the workshop are 29 proposals that are completely reframing the initial problem addressed by the City. From now on, there is much more than a bridge.

1 SCHOOL

319 STUDENTS

GRADUATE **+** UNDERGRADUATE **=**

Architecture
Landscape Architecture
Architectural History
Urban and Environmental Planning

Architecture
Architectural History
Urban and Environmental Planning

29 INTERDISPLINARY STUDENT TEAMS

34 FACULTY ADVISOR

1 NEW PROJECT TO BE **BUILT**

1 GUEST CRITIC **EDUARDO ARROYO**

10 DAYS

1 CITY

3,000 COMMUNITY VISITORS

5 WINNERS

4

MADRID, SPAIN

UNIVERSITY OF VIRGINIA
CHARLOTTESVILLE, VIRGINIA

01.30.12　　　　02.01.12　　　　02.03.12　　　　02.04.12　　　02.05.12　　　02.0

SITE VISIT

STUDIO WORK

Site Plan
Site Model
Diagrams
Perspective
Proposal At

CULBRETH THEATER

BELMONT

Teams 1-15　　　Teams 16-29

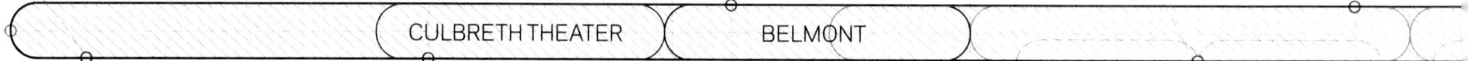

PUBLIC LECTURE

Eduardo Arroyo:
Buiding Uncertainties

KICK-OFF PANEL

Frank Stoner: Architect, Developer Belmont Lofts
Greg Jackson: Architect, Belmont Neighborhood Assoc Resident and BCNA President
Genevieve Keller: Architectural Historian and Preservation Planner
Elizabeth Meyer: Landscape Architect, Associate Professor Landscape Architecture
Robert F. Stroh: Co-Chair Downtown Business Association of Charlottesville
James Tolbert: Director Neighborhood Development Services
Satyendra Huja: Urban Planner, City Mayor
Kathy Galvin: Architect + City Council Member

GUEST CRITIQUE I

Eduardo Arroyo
NO.MAD

BELMONT BRIDGE, BELMONT

SCHOOL OF ARCHITECTURE
CAMPBELL HALL

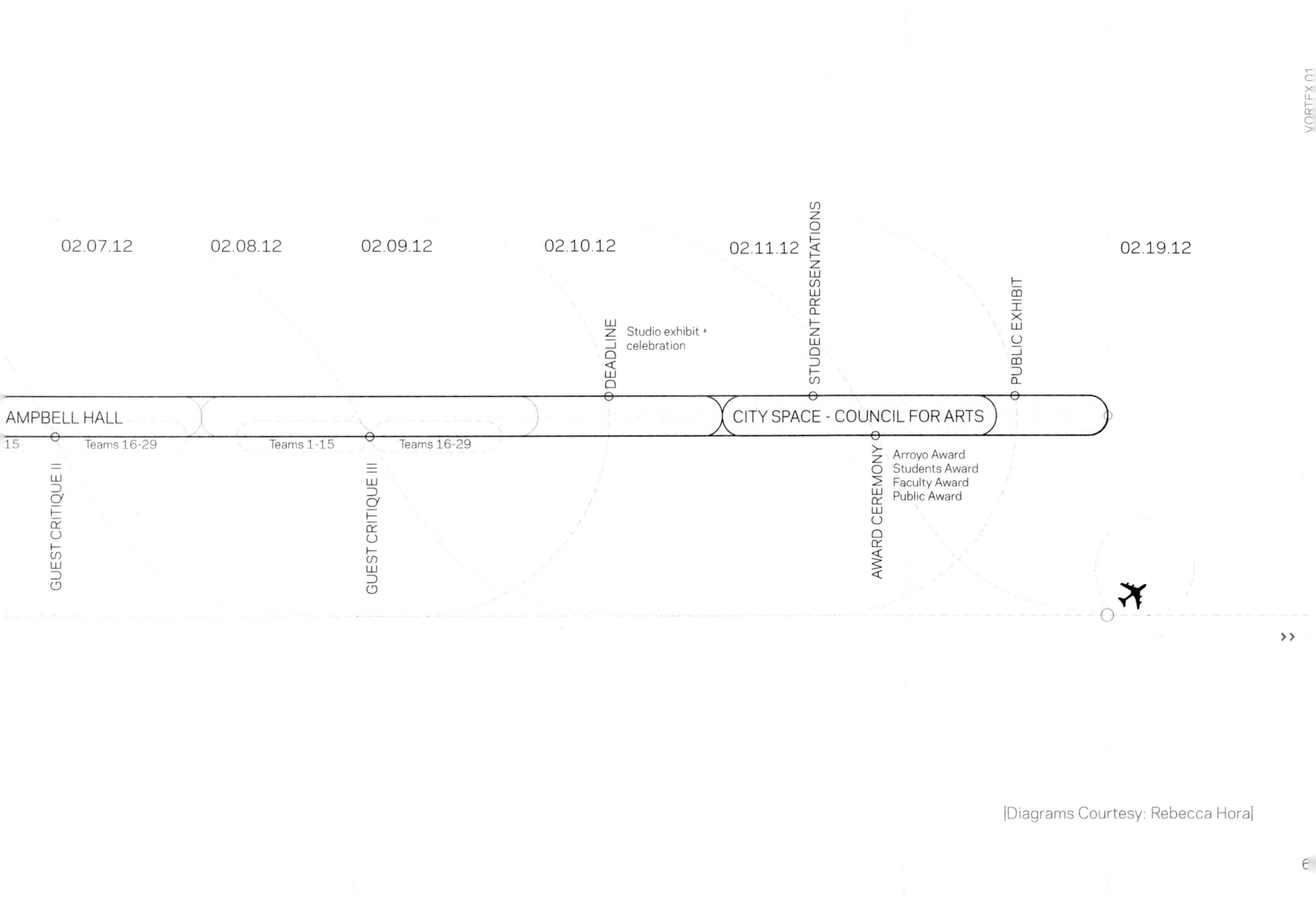

02.07.12   02.08.12   02.09.12   02.10.12   02.11.12   02.19.12

STUDENT PRESENTATIONS

DEADLINE — Studio exhibit + celebration

PUBLIC EXHIBIT

AMPBELL HALL   CITY SPACE - COUNCIL FOR ARTS

15   Teams 16-29   Teams 1-15   Teams 16-29

GUEST CRITIQUE II

GUEST CRITIQUE III

AWARD CEREMONY
Arroyo Award
Students Award
Faculty Award
Public Award

[Diagrams Courtesy: Rebecca Hora]

BELMONT BRIDGE

CHARLOTTESVILLE, VIRGINIA

Main Street before the pedestrian operation of the Downtown
Mall by Lawrence Halprin, circa 1971. [Photo Courtesy: Ed Roseberry]

Belmont Bridge, Downtown Charlottesville, circa 1961.
[Photo Courtesy: Ed Roseberry]

Belmont Bridge, Downtown Charlottesville, circa 1951.
[Photo Courtesy: Ed Roseberry]

Downtown Charlottesville traffic scheme; circa 1919.
[Drawings Courtesy: Automobile Blue Book Pub. Co.]

RUGBY ROAD

UNIVERSITY
AVENUE

WEST MAIN STREET

PARK STREET

MAIN STREET MALL

**BELMONT
BRIDGE**

VON STREET

ESSENTIAL COMPLEXITY / COMPLEJIDAD ESENCIAL

EDUARDO ARROYO, JAQUELIN T. ROBERTSON
VISITING PROFESSOR

The rich lexical expressiveness of the Spanish language allows its speakers to employ words whose meaning, in colloquial usage, may appear to be superficial; on the deeper linguistic level, however, these words actually define opposing entities and properties. For example, complejo (complex) and complicado (complicated) or simple (plain) and sencillo (simple) are used colloquially in a non-contrastive way, but when their adjectival variants refer to living entities, the latter forms acquire a more profound meaning. Thus, there may be a plain or a simple person, and a complicated or a complex person. Native speakers of Spanish consider plain and complicated to be negative personality traits, and simple and complex to be positive, although antagonistic, attributes which are characteristic of interesting people. These properties can easily be extrapolated and can be interpreted in a straightforward manner in the architectural domain. There may be, for example, plain architectures of a vulgar nature that may want to pass for simple, or complicated styles of sticky properties ['sticky properties' doesn't sound right to me, but I can't come up with anything else] that may pretend to be complex. Our essential task in the twenty-first century is to be able to discriminate among these architectures.

Part of this detective work consists of discriminating, on the one hand, between the introduction of the complication and the discovery of the complexity, and, on the other hand, to recognize the difference between the various degrees of deficiency of the plain and the innocuousness of the simple. The Complex entails the sum of a set of properties that

La riqueza léxica del castellano permite manejar palabras cuyo uso cotidiano es asimilable pero que con una mirada menos superficial definen caracteres y propiedades totalmente opuestos. Así, complejo y complicado o simple y sencillo se usan coloquialmente de manera alternativa pero su adjetivación a las personas les dota de su sentido profundo. Podremos tener, por tanto, una persona simple o una persona sencilla y una persona complicada o una persona compleja. La mayoría entendemos que simple y complicado son atributos negativos de la personalidad mientras que sencillo y complejo, aún siendo antagónicos, son atributos positivos de personas interesantes. Estas propiedades son fácilmente extrapolables y comprensibles en términos arquitectónicos. Habrá, por tanto, arquitecturas simples de carácter vulgar que intentan camuflarse de sencillas o, arquitecturas complicadas de propiedades empastadas que querrán aparentar complejas. La labor primordial de todos en el siglo XXI es saber diferenciarlas.

Una parte de esa labor detectivesca consiste en diferenciar la introducción de la complicación frente al descubrimiento de la complejidad e idénticamente en sus grados de adelgazamiento de la sencillez frente a la inocuidad de lo simple. Lo Complejo se muestra como una suma de propiedades que conforman un todo y lo hacen trascender hacia algo más elevado. También se nos aparece como la solución a un problema por medio de la averiguación. Lo Complicado sin embargo, se conforma mediante la suma de

produces a whole, and transcends it, moving it to a higher level. It also reveals itself as a solution that can be reached through investigation. The Complicated, however, is made up of the sum of various non-complementary properties, which generates both dispersion and confusion in the broader perspective. It also appears as the creation of additional problems while those at hand are still being resolved.

The Simple is that which has been stripped of all that is unnecessary, and whose result still preserves its intrinsic properties; it is the result of a subtraction. It comes as no surprise that it is the most difficult trip ever to be undertaken by the person, thus by architecture as a discipline. In contrast, the Plain lacks movement; it is an empty static system where nothing new appears, and where no existing trait is resolved. It is mere appearance.

Among the great discoveries of hidden properties that functioned before they were discovered by human beings is the double spiral of DNA and the revealed complexity of its processes of manipulation. Furthermore, watches are among the greatest designs that helped solve existing problems in our immediate reality. Presently, these objects allow us to control and relate to our environment in a more precise way. A watch-type complication implies any signifier that is added to the time paradigm; minutes and seconds, for example, lunar phases and time zones. However, automatic cords or devices used to eliminate rhythmical differences caused by gravitational forces, such as the

diversas propiedades no complementarias generando dispersión y confusión en el todo. También se presenta por la creación de nuevos problemas mientras intentamos resolver otro ya presente.

Lo Sencillo es aquello que se ha desprendido de lo no necesario preservando sus propiedades intrínsecas y por tanto es un trayecto al que se llega por sustracción. No es de extrañar que sea el viaje más difícil de la personalidad y por ende de la arquitectura. Por el contrario, en lo Simple no hay movimiento, es un sistema estático donde nada hay, nada nuevo aparece y nada existente se resuelve. Es pura apariencia.

Entre los grandes descubrimientos de propiedades de lo oculto que ya funcionaban antes de nuestra mirada está la doble espiral de ADN y la complejidad descubierta en torno ella para los procesos de su manipulación. Por otro lado, entre los grandes diseños para resolver problemas existentes de la realidad tangible están los relojes. Son objetos no existentes anteriormente y que nos permiten controlar y relacionarnos con nuestro entorno de una manera más precisa.

Una complicación relojera es toda aquella indicación que se añade a la de la hora, los minutos y los segundos, como por ejemplo, las fases lunares o los husos horarios. Sin embargo, la cuerda automática o los dispositivos utilizados para anular las diferencias de marcha en posiciones verticales generadas por la fuerza de la gravedad, como el "tourbillon" o el carrusel, no ofrecen una indicación propiamente

'tourbillon' or the carrousel, —are not in themselves signifiers. These mechanisms allow us to solve complex problems without adding new functions to them; this is why we treat them as complexities.

Complications add new layers of information and function; they are additive. Complexities increase and resolve the precision of pre-existing functions without adding new layers of information; they are multiplicative.

The carrousel and the 'tourbillon' have been designed to compensate for the effects of existing gravitational forces within the oscillatory precision of the spiral pivoting mount and the watch escape, thus voiding the deceleration and acceleration caused by the earth's pulling [gravitationall?] forces. The 'tourbillon' compensates for the function errors by locking the pivoting mount in a rotational gearbox; this offers extraordinary functional precision. This mechanism, which makes one rotation on its axis per minute, successively adopts all vertical positions, thus compensating for and eliminating any acceleration and deceleration. Likewise, a mechanism consisting of an automatic cord solves a practical problem; the watch's energy loss, transforming the kinetic energy of the user into cumulative static energy, which is consumed at a consistent rate by the spiral cord mechanism.

A watch that only gives hours, minutes and seconds, with the 'tourbillon' that liberates the watch from the earth's gravitational forces, becomes

dicha. Estos mecanismos resuelven grandes problemas sin añadir nuevas funciones y podemos considerarlos como complejidades. Las complicaciones añaden capas de información y función, son aditivas. Las complejidades aumentan y resuelven la precisión de funciones que ya existen sin añadir nuevas capas de información, son multiplicativas.

El carrusel y el "tourbillon" han sido pensados para compensar los efectos de la gravedad en la precisión oscilatoria del balancín-espiral y el escape de los relojes, anulando los efectos de ralentización y aceleración causados por la atracción terrestre. El "tourbillon" compensa los errores de funcionamiento encerrando el balancín en una caja giratoria que proporciona una extraordinaria precisión de funcionamiento. Este mecanismo, que realiza una rotación sobre sí mismo cada minuto, adopta sucesivamente todas las posiciones verticales compensando y anulando los efectos de aceleración y ralentización. Igualmente, el mecanismo de cuerda automática resuelve un problema práctico de pérdida de energía del reloj transformando la energía cinética del usuario en energía estática acumulada, consumida de manera consistente por el mecanismo de cuerda espiral.

Un reloj que sólo da las horas, minutos y segundos, con un "tourbillon" que le libera de la gravedad terrestre, es un objeto que ya puede estar en cualquier sitio y no depende por tanto del lugar, sólo del tiempo. Con una precisión de ese calibre dicho objeto ha resuelto

an object that may be placed anywhere: It does not depend on place anymore, only on time. With such precision, this object has solved the most fundamental problems, it has eliminated complications, and it has liberated itself from the environment. Nothing else can be taken away from it without damaging its performance. Therefore, only when a complexity has been accepted, assimilated, and clarified to the limit can we claim that an object's essence has revealed itself. Only then can we speak of an 'essentially complex' object.

In 1986, Fred Brooks established, in the Software Engineering realm, a distinction between Essential Complexity and Accidental Complexity, claiming that most engineers did not devote themselves to what should be essential, and that every problem reduction practice did not correlate with any improvements. He defined Accidental Complexity as the problems we create on our own, for example, the aspects of text writing or the optimization of code mounting. On the other hand, he defined Essential Complexity as that which was caused by the solving of the problem itself; considered essential for resolution of the problem and impossible to discard. In his search for the essential, Brooks advocated for an organic form of software development by way of an incremental model. This type of programming called 'agile development' functioned with a different operating system for each production stage, thus treating programming as a creative process composed of correlative phases. Based on these principles, high-end languages

los problemas fundamentales, ha eliminado las complicaciones y se ha liberado del entorno. Ya no se le puede quitar nada más sin dañar su funcionamiento. Podemos afirmar que su esencia ha aparecido cuando la complejidad ha sido aceptada, asimilada y precisada hasta el límite. Podemos hablar de un objeto "esencialmente complejo".

En 1986, Fred Brooks hizo una distinción entre la Complejidad Esencial y la Accidental en la Ingeniería de Software afirmando que la mayoría de los ingenieros ya no se dedicaba a lo esencial por lo que todas las actividades de reducción de los grandes problemas no producían ninguna mejora. En sus reflexiones definía la Complejidad Accidental como aquella que se refiere a los problemas que creamos por nosotros mismos, por ejemplo, los detalles de la escritura o la optimización de montaje de códigos. Por otro lado, definía la Complejidad Esencial como la causada por el problema en sí al ser resuelto entendida como algo imprescindible para su resolución y que nada puede eliminar.

Brooks abogaba en esa búsqueda de lo esencial por un crecimiento orgánico del software a través de un desarrollo incremental. Un tipo de programación denominada "desarrollo ágil" que proporciona un sistema de trabajo diferente para cada etapa productiva configurando la programación como un proceso creativo de fases correlativas. Desde esa óptica, una tecnología que hizo una mejora significativa en el ámbito de la complejidad esencial fue la invención de lenguajes

such as Fortran were invented, and this type of technology significantly improved the realm of Essential Complexity. Today, innovative languages such as C ++ or Java are only considered accidental improvements made to the original language form.

Essential Complexity never complains about the complex as life's primary characteristic; it tries to reduce the factors associated with it to the absolute minimum in order for them to be solved. Essential complexity is not yet another attribute of urban reality; it is its reality. Given that the spaces in which we exist continue to present unsolved problems, we assume that the solution to them must involve an attack on the core of their existing complications. Similarly, it is also true that we can camouflage a resulting state with instantaneous tranquilizing elements of a plain appearance; however, time will eventually make visible the analgesic property of these tranquilizing elements and will reveal their true virulent sickness. Just in the same way that most people take an aspirin instead of going to the doctor in order to pretend that nothing is wrong with them, so are our cities' urban complications camouflaged by political delights lacking any active property—other than the ephemeral magic spell that generates them. Maybe that is the reason why popular elections not rooted in previous collective processes are so very harmful for a city, whether it be it in Scandinavia, Switzerland, Virginia or Timbuktu.

de alto nivel, como el Fortran. Hoy en día los nuevos idiomas, tales como C ++ o Java se consideran solo mejoras accidentales.

La complejidad esencial no reniega nunca del carácter primordial de la vida, lo complejo, mientras intenta reducir los factores de la misma al mínimo imprescindible para su resolución. No es un atributo más de nuestra actualidad urbana, es su realidad. Puesto que los lugares en los que actuamos siguen teniendo problemas sin resolver suponemos que la solución ha de atacar el corazón de su complicación. Es cierto que podemos disimular el resultado con elementos de carácter tranquilizador, calmantes instantáneos de apariencia simple, pero el tiempo negará su propiedad analgésica para volver a mostrar la enfermedad en toda su virulencia. Al igual que la mayoría de las personas prefieren tomar una aspirina antes de ir al médico y pretender que no ocurre nada, en nuestras ciudades vemos cada vez más esa actitud de ocultación de las complicaciones urbanas con golosinas políticas sin ninguna propiedad activa excepto la de un hechizo popular momentáneo. Quizás por ello las votaciones populares no involucradas en los desarrollos previos son tan extremadamente dañinas para la ciudad, en Escandinavia, en Suiza, en Virginia o en Tombuctú.

La pregunta que nos deberíamos hacer los arquitectos del presente sería, ¿Cuales serían los "tourbillones" y los "sistemas de desarrollo ágil" a implementar para fabricar arquitecturas esencialmente complejas? Esta pregunta fue la que guió el Taller

The question that we contemporary architects should be asking ourselves is this: What are the 'tourbillons' and the 'agile development systems' that need to be implemented in order for us to construct essentially complex architectures? This question led the workshop I directed at UVA, where my objective was to go beyond the quick, local, urban-oriented competition surrounding the Belmont Bridge project and stimulate a profound investigation of the issue. This objective allowed for students to immerse themselves in the still unknown, uncomfortable world of the Essentially Complex. It was probably a special place and moment in time for architects to bid for proposals that, distancing themselves from the banal, helped solve great urban mysteries. My most sincere gratitude and admiration to the students and professors who walked (could be "accompanied me ") with me and shared, during that adventure, their courage and strength.

que dirigí en la UVA tratando de provocar una investigación más profunda que la de un expeditivo concurso local de ideas urbanas para Bellmont Bridge. Con ella se impulsó una inmersión de los estudiantes en ese mundo todavía desconocido e incómodo de la Complejidad Esencial. Probablemente se trató de un lugar especial en el tiempo para apostar por proposiciones que huyendo de lo banal nos ayuden a resolver las grandes incógnitas urbanas. A todos los estudiantes y profesores que quisieron acompañarme con su valentía y solidez en aquella aventura les dedico mi más sincera admiración y agradecimiento.

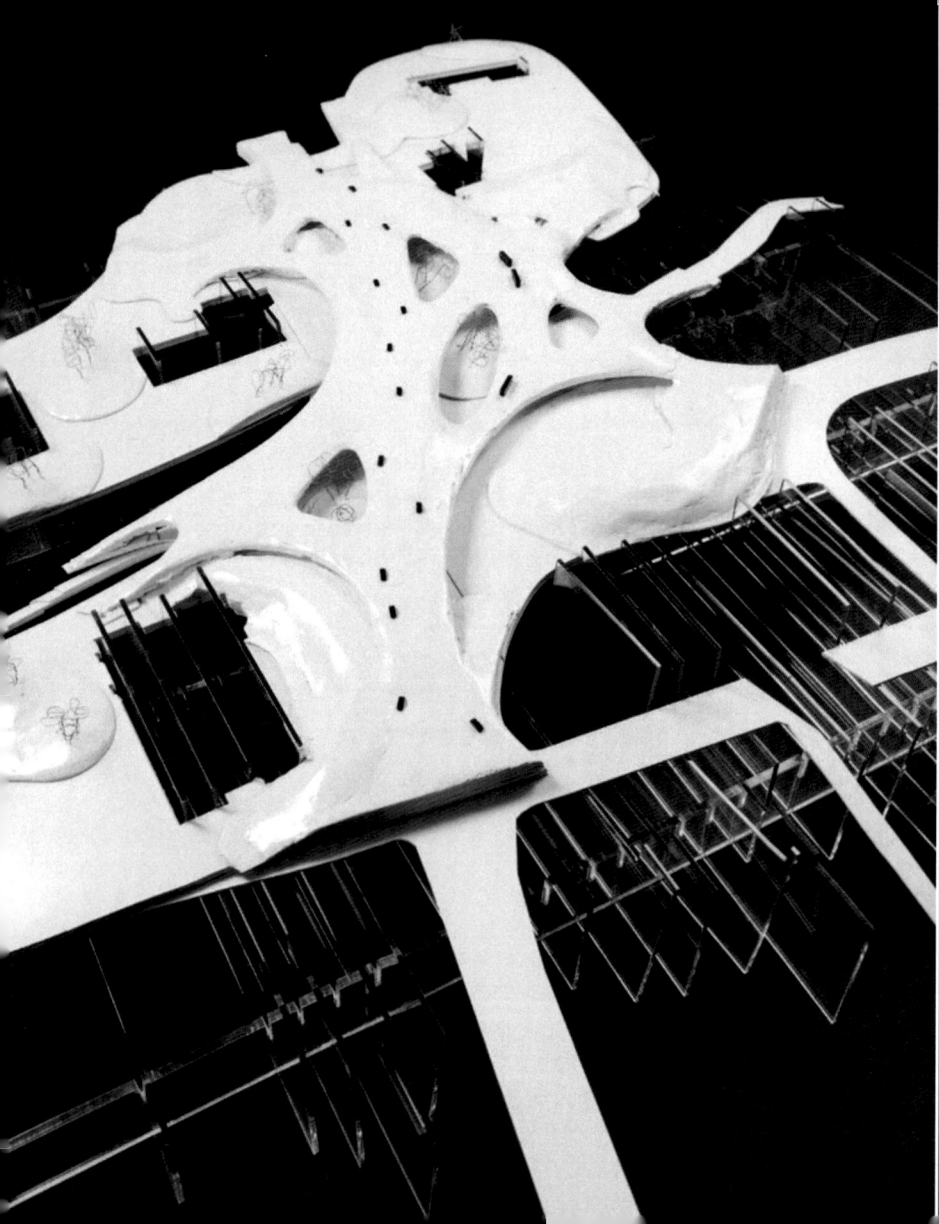
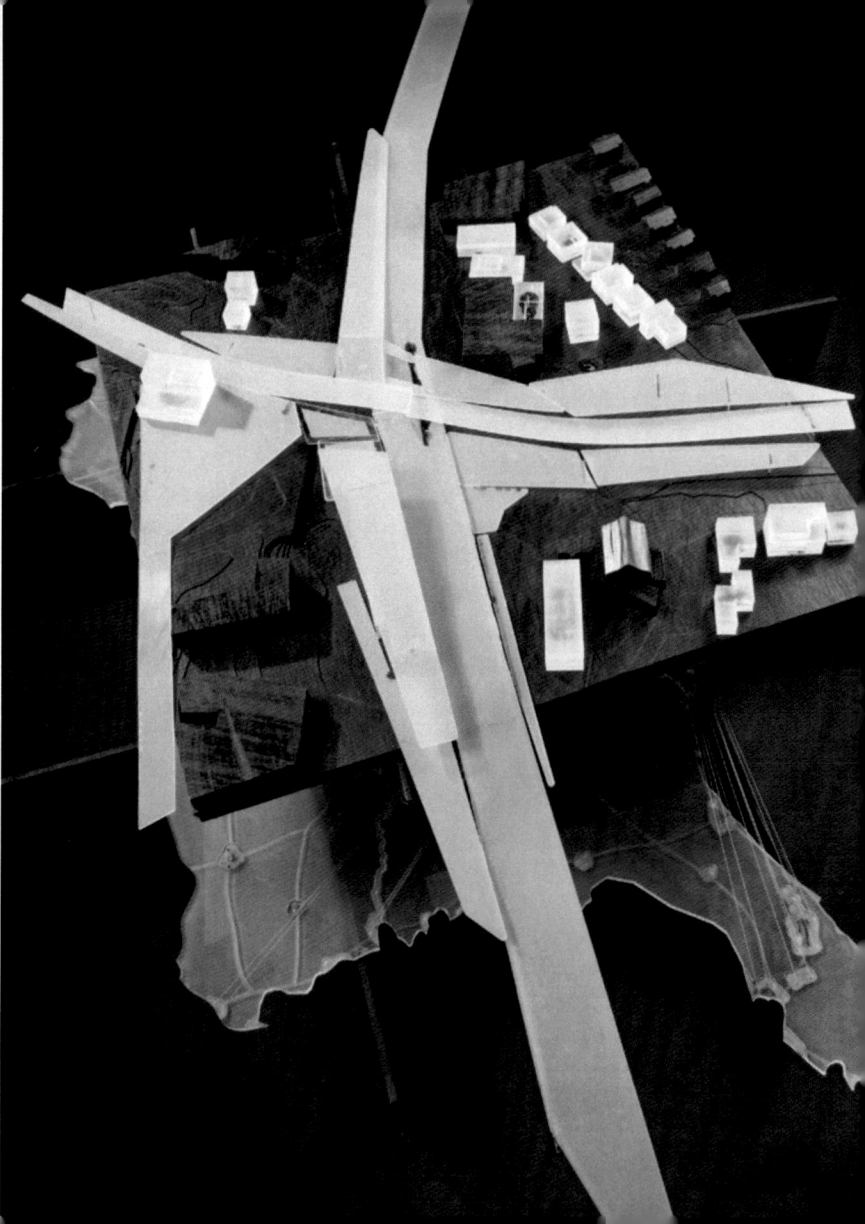

WINNING PROPOSALS

ARROYO AWARD
HUB STEP

"After a very intense and exciting workshop, the decision of the Arroyo's Prize has been very intentionally done. I have chosen the project of HUB STEP, because of the level of exploration and compromise towards a borader view of city connectivity. It expresses urban continuit both in terms of programs and infrastructues, as well as the creation of new public space. So architecture and landscape work together." [Eduardo Arroyo]

PUBLIC AWARD
BELMONT UNABRIDGED

FACULTY AWARD
MINI BRIDGE, MEGA CONNECTOR
SUDDEN FOREST

STUDENT AWARD
BELMONT PARKWAY

[Photos Courtesy: Scott Smith]

HUB STEP

We understand the bridge as a surface of collective experience - an activated public space that builds upon the ideology of the Halprin's vision for the Charlottesville Downtown Mall. The Belmont Bridge is envisioned as an extension of the public space of the mall – a continuous urban surface supporting fluid connections across the railroad as well as creating spaces of exchange above and below. This landscape supports a non-hierarchical experience where pedestrians, bikes, cars and public transportation move across a shared surface. The co-existence of different modes of circulation thus becomes a public act, one which engenders new connections and relationships across the City of Charlottesville and the greater region. The local and regional transportation networks of Charlottesville are currently egregiously disjointed. Centralizing the various transit modes that connect and support the citizens of Charlottesville provides the opportunity for the bridge to act as an intermodal transit hub. This will be the new threshold to the city, sited at a crucial juncture in the urban fabric, where one arrives via regional transportation and immediately accesses local networks of buses, trolleys, bikes and pedestrian paths.

As a continuation of the Mall, the surface bridge peels up to become a landscape of native grassland hillocks crisscrossed by local transport routes. This landscape also wraps in on itself, sheltering spaces below for a larger regional transit terminal and its associated social and commercial activities. The lifted urban crust is punctured by large elliptical apertures that foster vertical exchanges between transport modes, social activity, and light. These connect the experience of the sunny grassland above to that of the shaded forest below. The spaces therefore emerge from the folded surface, engage one another, and provide a collective experience of movement. The resulting landscape is one of multiplicity, where our quotidian activities are enriched by complexity, connectivity, and the experience of difference.

ADVISOR: Margarita Jover; TEAM: Katherine Ling Lai , Brianna Dobbs, Victor Azevedo , Xavier Scipio, Tyler Whitney, Cassidy Wolfe, Wattana Savanh, Paul Golisz, Maureen McGee, Abigail Whelan, Kurt Marsh

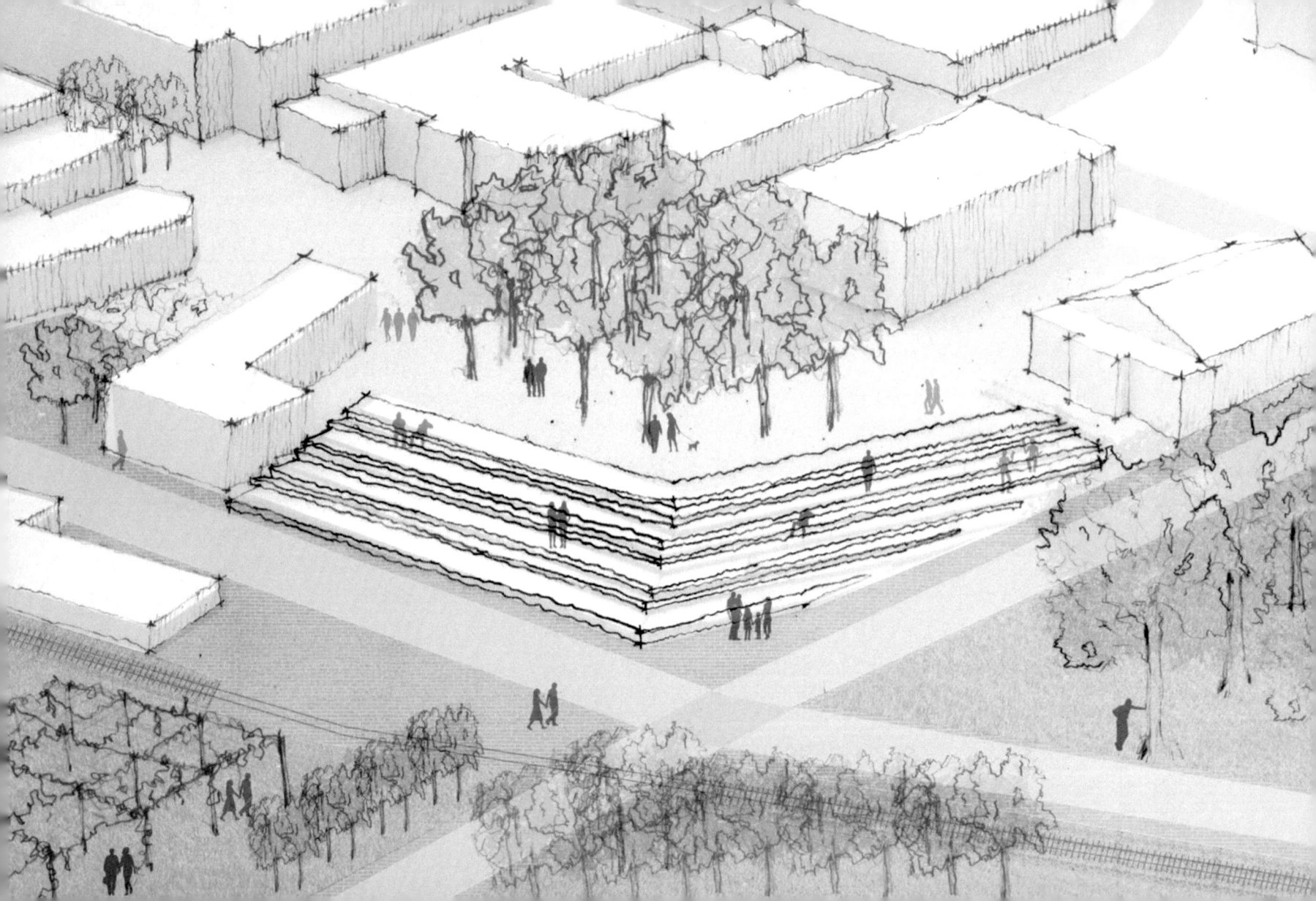

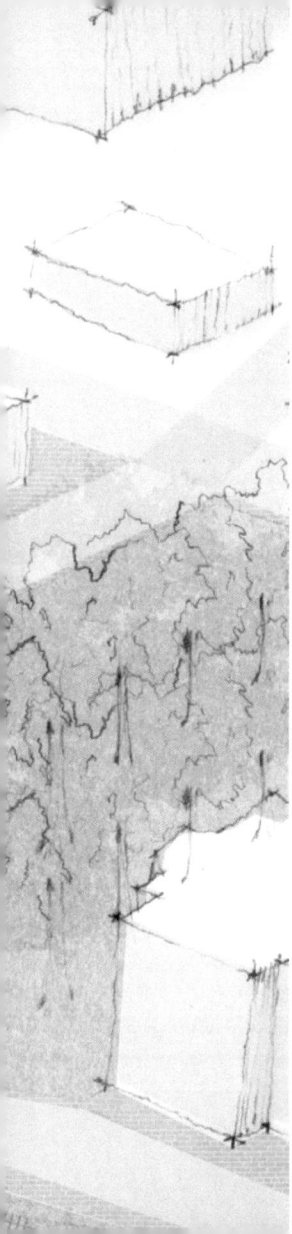

BELMONT UNABRIDGED

Our idea is to connect the Downtown Mall with Belmont and views beyond of Jefferson's Monticello Mountain and the Southwest Mountains. In order to do this we have created a civic plaza with broad terraces leading to a vibrant new farmers' market located on the Belmont side of the railroad tracks. On the plaza is a new bosque of willow oak trees, extending Lawrence Halprin's beautiful pedestrian mall groves, while completing his unrealized vision for an east end plaza. The new farmers' market incorporates the iconic flour mill (Beck-Cohen) where local farmers historically brought their harvest.

We seek an optimistic act of urban place-making, gateway, connection, and recovery. The design drops the Belmont Bridge roadway to a narrower grade-level railroad crossing. It moves the Pavilion Tent to a more historically and environmentally appropriate place. At the former IX factory, where thousands of Charlottesville workers produced silk parachutes that helped win World War II, we propose a new billowing performance tent. Located in a low-lying valley the tent is bounded by earthen protectors and Oakwood Cemetery to dampen concert noise. This location aligns on axis with the Downtown Mall's Central Place and extends recent urban developments along South Second Street. We do not need the proposed $14.5 million bridge; historically over 100 trains moved daily through this area. Now the number is often only 5 trains a day, taking less than 7 minutes to pass. We propose widening the nearby 4th Street underpass to two lanes. When trains approach downtown, signals can direct traffic to the underpass and west to the bridge at Ridge Street. Land recovered from the bridge right-of-way and approaches will provide excellent sites for new dwellings and businesses. By UnAbridging we will strengthen our neighborhoods and our city.

ADVISORS: WG Clark, Daniel Bluestone; TEAM: Jason Levi Truesdale, Enrique Cavelier, Charlotte Rose Miller, Nancy Ellen Connors, Roderick Paul Cruz, Wyatt Hill, Meghan Maupin, Christopher Barker, Kate Martin, Kelly Hitzing, Joanna McNnight, KirstenSparenborg, Madeleine Hawks

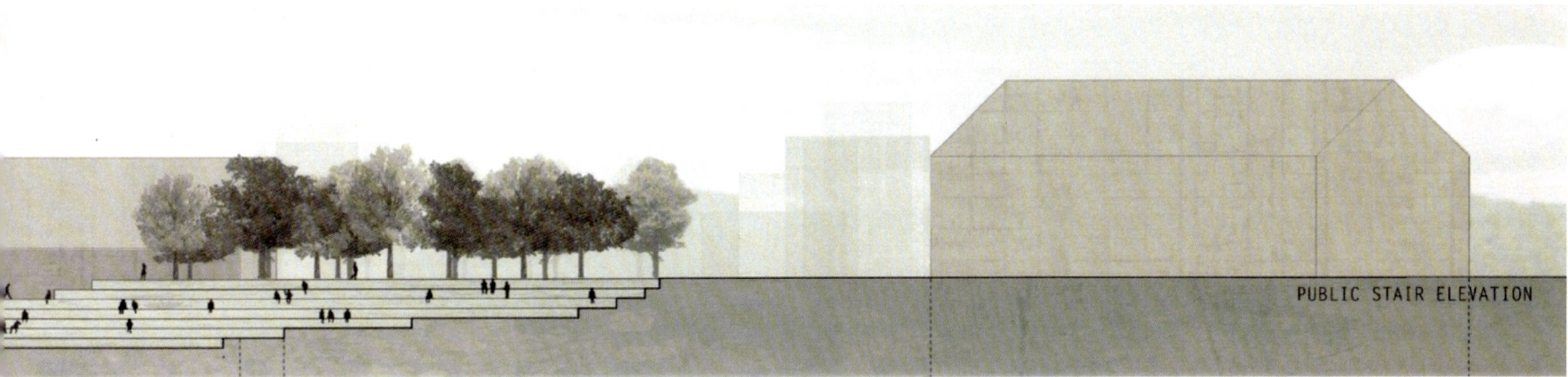

PUBLIC STAIR ELEVATION

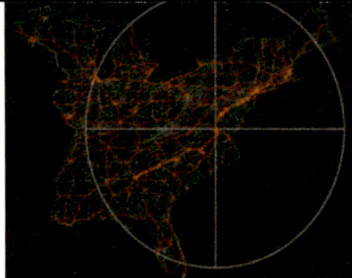
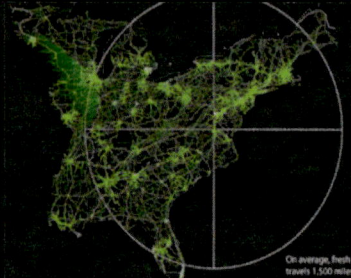

On average, fresh produce travels 1,500 miles before it reaches the supermarket.

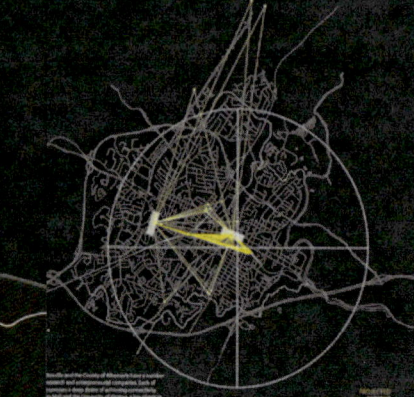
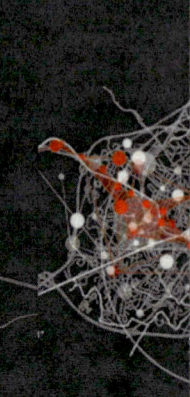

Charlottesville has a growing market for local produce, with several local farms participating.

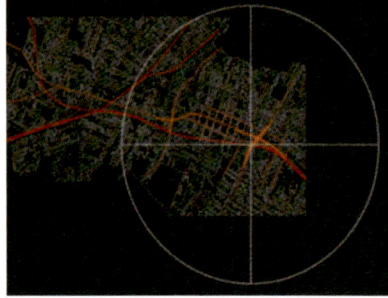

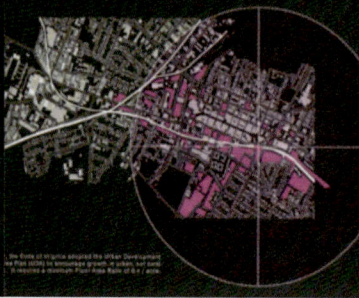
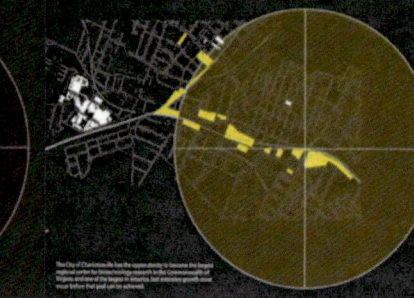

TRANSPORTATION   FOOD PRODUCTION/DISTRIBUTION   DENSITY   TECH INDUSTRY

MINI BRIDGE, MEGA CONNECTOR

The Mega Connector redefines the Belmont Bridge as not just a physical structure, but as a structure for change, expanding the Downtown Mall and establishing a new gateway to the city. The design anticipates a larger urban strategy, intervening as a catalyst for growth, civic participation, and forming new identities for Charlottesville. Our initial design move entails lowering the railroad below ground from Ridge Street to Mead Avenue to eliminate the necessity for multiple levels of infrastructure above grade. This presents an opportunity to expand the downtown territory and its linkages where the railroad had divided it. The new territory acts as a multifaceted continuation of the Downtown Mall in several directions and on multiple levels. It functions as a park, a civic space, a farmer's market, a venue for outdoor events and an expansion of Charlottesville's downtown towards Belmont. Our second design move reinstates the old C&O train station downtown as Charlottesville's primary train station. The current station is in a heterotopic landscape, neither downtown nor near the University. We propose reclaiming the station back into the historic downtown station, connecting it into a new below-grade platform as well as into the transformed above-grade linear park. Positioning the station downtown will benefit Charlottesville in multiple ways: bringing more visitors downtown and bolstering the city's economy, density and connections with nearby towns. The Mega Connector will forge connections on multiple scales, including Charlottesville's connection to the greater region and its past. The southwest corner of the current bridge, for example, was once an industrial territory, and our design proposes that new 21st century industries such as biotech centers will move into the abandoned quadrant. The processes and programs that extend from the bridge will set into motion a restructuring far beyond the extents of the site: through Charlottesville and the entire region.

1 BELOW-GRADE RAIL

2 ESTABLISH LINEAR PARK

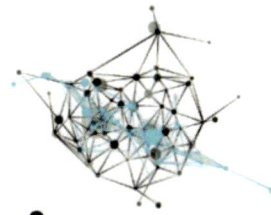

3 FORGE CONNECTIVITY

4 CATALYZE CHANGE

ADVISOR: Nana Last; TEAM: Christopher Wertman, Lu Xu, Robert Grooms II, Yujing Han, Jude Ghassan Majali, Eric Kuhn, David Matthews, Andrew Milner, katherine Treppendahl, Dasha Lebedeva, Charles Sparkman

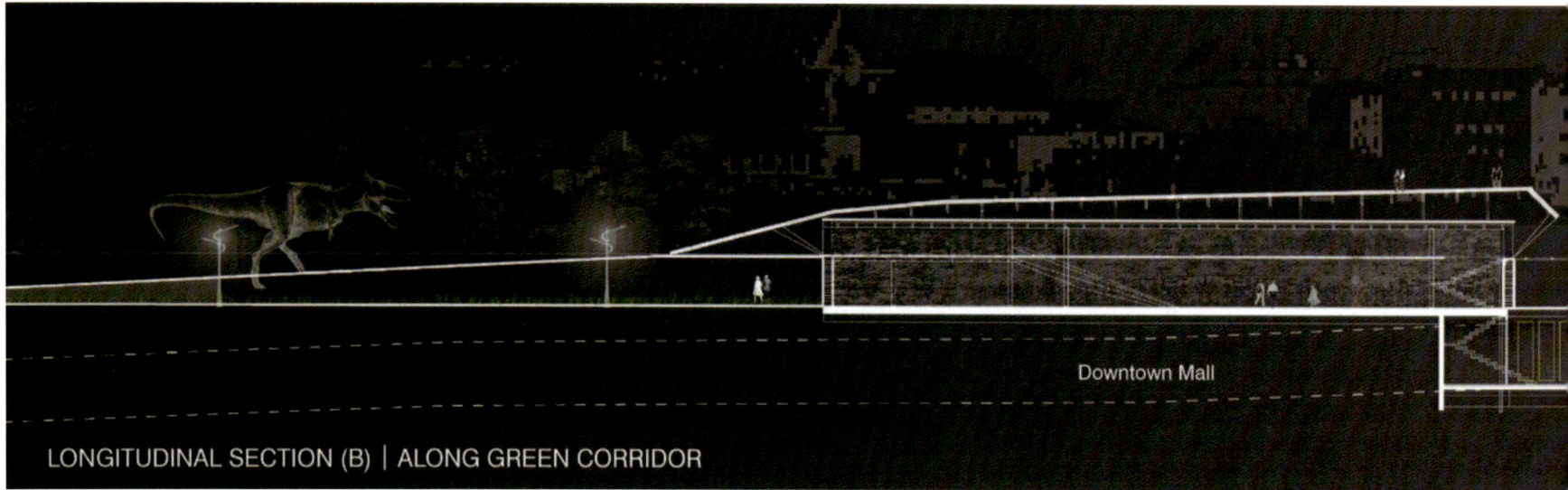

LONGITUDINAL SECTION (B) | ALONG GREEN CORRIDOR

Downtown Mall

view down Water St. looking toward new train station

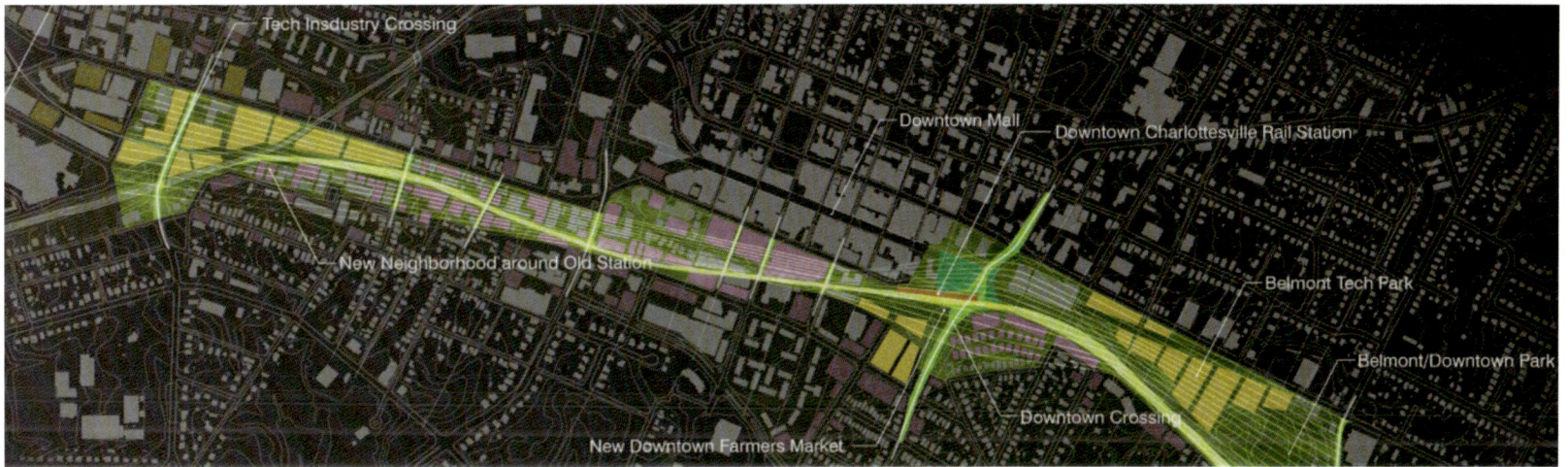

Tech Insdustry Crossing

Downtown Mall

Downtown Charlottesville Rail Station

New Neighborhood around Old Station

Belmont Tech Park

Belmont/Downtown Park

Downtown Crossing

New Downtown Farmers Market

The bridge & subterranean train station catalyze new development along the old rail corridor.

SUDDEN FOREST

A bridge is a singular object, bridging is an act of connecting. The desire to reconnect neighborhoods separated by scalar changes in the transportation infrastructure of Charlottesville is one that cannot be addressed in a singular manner. As such we have proposed a system of bridging that creates new urban spaces and affects the existing urban fabric. Our proposal advises three bridging strategies for adapting Charlottesville's existing railway: spatial, infrastructural and experiential. Though these play out at multiple locations throughout the city, we will highlight how theses work on the Downtown/Belmont site. We have proposed the creation of 5 forests in the city. These act as spatial and programmatic connections between two or more neighborhoods. In each, pedestrian and bicycle traffic is privileged over vehicular. On our site this necessitates the creation of a tunnel under the existing railway to connect neighborhoods by car, and two pedestrian/cyclist bridges that connect through the forest.

The forest itself is a densely packed space modeled on the Jefferson and George Washington Forests in Virginia and Kentucky with an 80% / 20% ratio of hardwoods to conifers. The forest accommodates some public open space and amenities including housing the covered music pavilion.

The forest occupies a ground plane that is disconnected from its surroundings, forming a programmed edge. These programs are situated under the forest, accessed at street level and zoned for mixed use and commercial, impacting each neighborhood differently.

Vehicular connections across the railway are increased throughout the city, as bridges and tunnels provide multiple connection to many separated neighborhoods. Pedestrian connections take the form of delicately constructed bridges that span the gulf created by the railway, elevating pedestrian into the tree canopy and providing views into the valley that Charlottesville inhabits. Each forest creates an experience of the city. The density and species selection of the trees produces mists, fragrances, sounds and textures that are set in juxtaposition to the industrial railway. The addition of forests into the city creates micro-climates that becoming eco-sinks for plants and animals. Along the edge of the forest, shops, dining and office space is created when there is a discrepancy in grade. The new venues look outward to the neighborhoods they connect, emphasizing the unique identities to each.

ADVISOR: Michael Beaman; TEAM: Arnold Ildoo Lee , Erin kelsey Tait , Brittany Jaye Harris , Charles Himes , Jamie Christine Epley, kathleen Smith, Matthew Steppan, Maria Arellano , Joey Hayes, Marie Miller, Tran Le

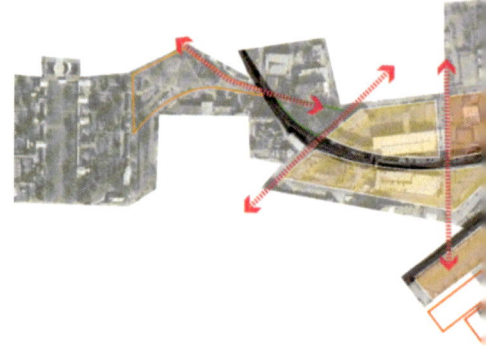

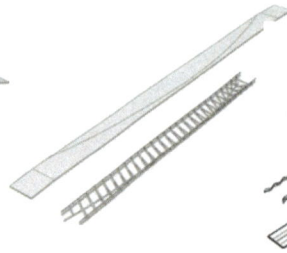

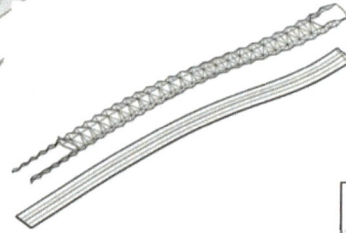

evolution of the plinth   split bridge   straight bridge   tunnel

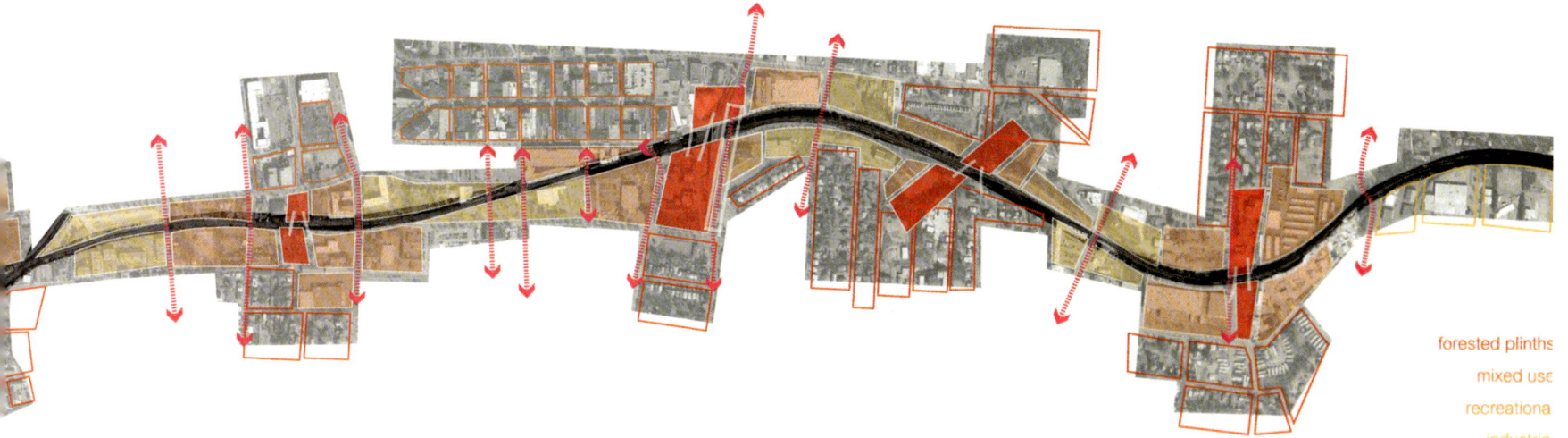

forested plinths
mixed use
recreational
industrial
existing commercial
existing residential
existing recreational

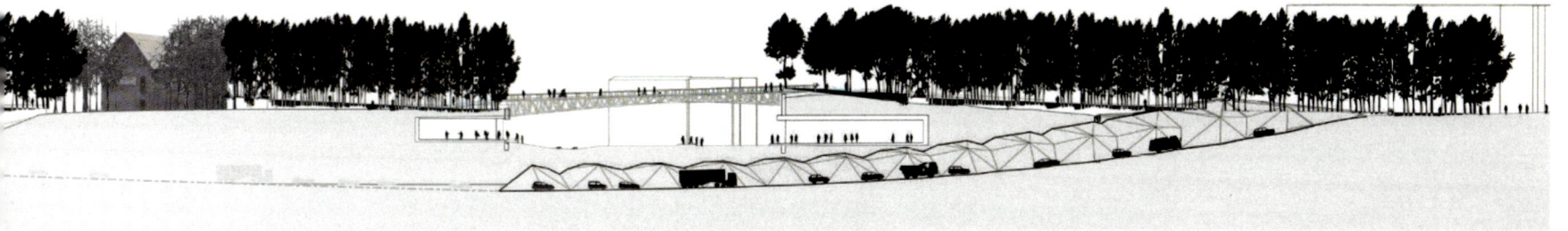

BELMONT PARKWAY

Belmont PARKway is a green oasis in the heart of Charlottesville that strengthens the connections between neighborhoods. This network of three parks is designed for transit, entertainment and leisure. Cars crossing the railroad tracks disappear under the parkway creating a safe environment for bicyclists and pedestrians above.

The Transit route offers a direct path from Belmont to the Charlottesville Transit Station and the Downtown Mall. A bike share gives residents the option to rent bikes to get to work. Along the entertainment parkway, one can view public art, listen to an intimate musical performance or sit on the slope of Charlottesville's new grassy pavilion and look out to Monticello. The leisure parkway allows pedestrians to take a stroll through the native gardens and enjoy lunch in a picnic grove. A grand public plaza anchors the intervention on the north side of the tracks.

On the Belmont side, the PARKway brings residents to the new home for Charlottesville's farmers' market. The market can either be set up under the green roofs offering protection from the elements or out in the sun on a summer day. Meanwhile, children can enjoy a new playground of fountains.

ADVISOR: Brad Schuck; TEAM: Kaitlin Gerson Marie, Tyler Austen Haley, Nicholas Levi Ratcliff, Aaron Michael Simon, Sonad Uygur, Jessica Vanecek, Callie Broaddus, katherine Cannella, Crystal Prigmore, Amelia Einbender-Lieber, Brian Flynn

OBSERVATIONS ON A BRIDGE

ROBIN DRIPPS, DAVID T. FITZGIBBON
PROFESSOR OF ARCHITECTURE

It was only a bridge, but as the two week competition unfolded, it became clear to everyone that they were engaged in a radical expansion of the field of architecture. It was not even obvious if architecture, at least as it is currently understood, was the most appropriate disciplinary territory. The thirty teams were already a hybrid consisting of students at all levels and from all of the distinct departments in the school (Architecture, Landscape Architecture, Architecture History, and Urban and Environmental Planning) so that the internal discussions were not constrained by disciplinary boundary. The site itself quickly lost any sense of bounds as well, whether this was spatial or temporal. Inexplicable fragments and other enigmatic anomalies were everywhere pointing farther and farther back in time to buried histories that, once unearthed, had to be included as part of the present context. Spatially, the local context was anything but locally constrained. Networks, vital to the economic, social, and political productivity of the region converged here, and yet failed to engage, leaving their distant origins only a remote presence. As the potential for local actions to promote regional interconnectivity became more apparent, teams recognized the influences that this would have locally and the opportunities it provided. Remnants of matrices and corridors essential for the large scale territorial connectivity that supports vegetative and animal habitat could be reconnected and reconfigured to provide the continuity necessary for all species to thrive. The bridge was a consequence of the railroad passing through this low point of the city. The rail was once an active participant in an important regional transport network. This earlier state provided opportunities that are no longer utilized. Present initiatives to bring back lost service could call for the one remaining rail station in town to move back to this crucial location, where it could become part of a multimodal transport infrastructure aggregating train, bus, taxi, bicycle, and pedestrians into the cultural life of the town. Might this become the bridge itself? But what if this last vestige of rail connectivity were to die? A look at the existing but underused rail right of ways reveals the possibility of a local light rail network that could link the expanding development in the surrounding counties as an alternate to some of the present initiatives for new highways. Finally, what if this amazing matrix of connectivity were to become an urban forest or productive park connecting to the nearby trail systems and thus bring a wild nature into the heart of urban culture? Water is a topical subject in Charlottesville because the town government fails to understand the interconnectivity of systems within the larger watershed and the resultant cycles of drought. The current bridge was constructed at a critical divide in the local watershed, obscuring some connective systems. Students discovered that roof water drainage combined with large areas of impermeable surfaces had the potential to contribute to the opposite outcome of excessive runoff eroding stream banks and destroying stream ecologies that once kept the mosquito population in balance. Taken together, these disparate pieces can be understood as potential parts of a new distributed network where natural

Previous Page: Robin Dripps, T. David Fitzgibbon Professor of Architecture in discussion with her student team. [Photos courtesy: Wimer]

process and products of human agency work together to create a far more effective ecology. The outcome would be a hybrid hydrological structure made up of roofs, ground, streams, pipes, and rivers where local and regional networks work together. This more inclusive definition of the structure of a watershed--where the contribution of buildings and large parts of urban infrastructure are included--shifts attention away from the initial project area in order to understand various scales of interdependence.

At best, architecture practices have succeeded in keeping water outside and therefore out of mind. When water is inside, it is understood differently. Pipes, faucets, and drains are an abstraction that is difficult to imagine connecting to natural process. Water arrives when the handle turns. But where has it come from and will it always arrive so predictably? And then, after use, where is it headed? The disconnect between natural processes and human artifice is huge. It seems that two completely different worlds coexist unaware of what each might offer to the other. Of course, this has not always been the case. Take, for example, the step wells of India, the fountains of Rome, or the remarkable landscapes in Tasmania constructed on the principles of permaculture. Here, the value of water has transcended simple instrumentality to become an interwoven presence within a complex cultural matrix. Perhaps this is what defines the capacity for a culture to sustain itself.

DESIGNING THE NEW URBAN GROUND

An immediate response to these hybrid systems was the realization: the long enduring trope that establishes an adversarial relationship between culture and nature or at best leaves these two without a relationship has not served either very well. It should be obvious to most that even after the heroically long project to bring understanding to the human condition by establishing an oppositional relationship with all that is otherwise that this is an artificial construct and one that has been detrimental to a necessarily productive relationship. With that barrier breached, all these disparate pieces seemed to aggregate around an idea of urban ground operating as a dense, thick, layered hybrid infrastructure variably responsive to the complex intersections of natural process and human artifice. Looking at the collected entries to the competition, it is possible to trace the origins of many of the component pieces back to the research and teaching of faculty members among all departments. These faculty had not had the chance until this competition to work in as intensely collaborative a mode as was possible with their surrogates-- the students--who carried these fragments of thought into the public arena of the competition team. The productive discourse that followed with all the necessary frictions and revelations make a compelling argument for rethinking much received wisdom about how a curriculum is constructed and how knowledge is understood in isolation.

COMMON THEMES

Design ought to begin with a critical reframing of the program. Here the bridge as a primary objective obscured a much broader set of connective possibilities. Once reframed as urban ground, the program unleashed its multilayered relational potential provoking searches for discontinuities, fissures, gaps, and other disruptions to the complex web of physical, ecological, social, and political interactions that define urban existence. This reframing produced a different set of lenses through which to inquire and develop ideas further. Weaving, sewing, and other active open ended fabric operations advanced this agenda better than static, unresponsive methods of control coming from master planning. Urban ground is extensive, boundless, and always in flux. Edges are continually under negotiation becoming a rich urban ecotone. Centers no longer hold hegemonic primacy as they shift, multiply, and divide to be subsumed within a dynamic urban field where flows of all kinds are valued over stasis. The idea of a city, along with its diagrammatic clarity—defining what ought to be included and what is best left outside--has proven to be a flawed model as its uncontrolled growth acts parasitically to destroy the host countryside that provides the resources for it to survive. Instead, the process of urbanization itself is being rethought to behave as an emergent, self-regulating organism where growth describes an increase in interconnectivity and complexity and therefore creates an inherently self-sustaining structure.

Students at work in Campbell Hall, University of Virginia School of Architecture. [Photos Courtesy: Wimer]

Within this emergent form of urbanization, it should be obvious that many forms of nature, including the human construction of landscapes, will be integral parts of the larger networks. Although some of these are already considered part of the urban project, others, such as forests and farms, have been kept outside, making their wholesale disappearance an inevitable outcome. But, even those pieces of landscape more familiar to the urban dweller, such as parks and gardens, will need to perform at a comparable level of interactive complexity by also becoming intensely hybridized so as to fulfill multiple roles in this new urban structure. The new bridge was intended to better link the downtown to an older working class suburb that has recently become gentrified. Aside from the problematic prior social and economic exclusions that this would bring up, the issue that was addressed by many of the teams was the nature of the suburb itself. Rather than continuing the opposition between city and suburb that any form of link suggested could not this emergent form of urbanization find value in parts of each so that intervention and growth might now provide the complex set of expectations that the best of these two worlds could provide. These are important beginnings to a much larger project. What is clear to everyone involved is the need to rethink how we work together in a world of increasing complexity so that these beginnings might find an equally exciting extended life.

STUDENT PROPOSALS

WILBR // WEB INFRASTRUCTURE LINKING BELMONT

CHARLOTTESVILLE GATEWAYS

ONCE UPON A TIME

WALK THE LINES

THE SQUISHY JOINT

C'VILL ACTIVE SURFACE

X-ING

WEAVE BRIDGE

MULTI-MODAL NEXUS

PATH PROGRAMS PLACE

THE CITY BRIDGE

BELMONT EXCHANGE

THE GRID, THE FLOUR MILL & THE LANDSCAPE LINE

BELLIVILLE // CONNECTING THE CITY & THE GRITTY

HUG IT OUT C'VILLE

BRIDGE OVER RUBBLED WATER

ENGAGEMENT AND PROXIMITY

CITY X-ING

THE LATENT VORTEX OF FLOW

GAITWAY LOOP

CIRCUS OF SPEEDS

THE CONFLUENCE

VORTEX CORTEX CONTEXT

THE BELMONT RIDGE

WILBR // WEB INFRASTRUCTURE LINKING BELMONT

WILBr is a system of elevated interweaving pathways that reconnect the communities of Belmont and Charlottesville. Our new urban ground provides the opportunity for multi-modal travel between Belmont and the downtown mall Using a combination of cables and concrete, WILBr rises above the terrain to foster urban development and densification. Our proposal uses a perforated and thickened urban ground to create layered connections and moments of pause. Multiple levels of new ground stitch together new and existing buildings within the same structure while enhancing moments of transition. The formation of a robust network of pathways, green spaces, and entrances on the inhabitable roof revitalizes the disjointed communities and provides unique experiences of the surrounding city and scenery. WILBr sews new running and bicycling trails into the existing railway corridor, providing multiple places to cross over. Resting at the intersection of all paths is the Charlottesville Farmer's Market. To the West lies mixed income residential buildings, and to the East a reinvigorated industrial infrastructure. The transition from the downtown to Belmont is reimagined to offer community and development opportunities while retaining the neighborhoods' distinct qualities. Where the current bridge cemented an automobile lifestyle and shattered the pedestrian life, WILBr sews the fragmented Charlottesville back together.

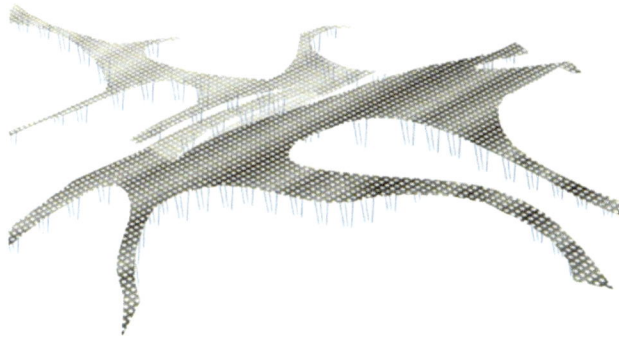

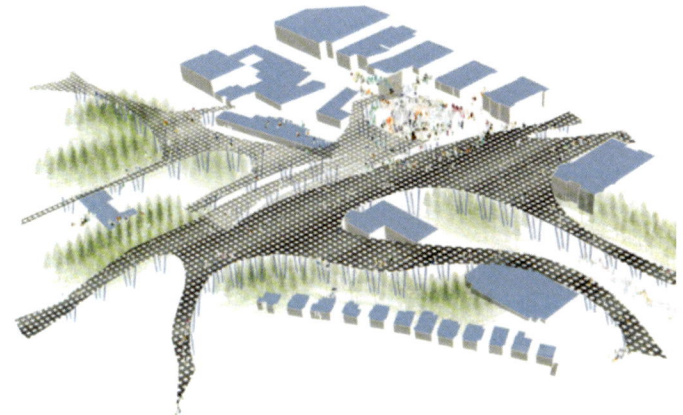

ADVISOR: Robin Dripps; TEAM: William Franklin Artrip IV, Max Elliot Cuttler, Adede Amenyah, Margaret Brigid Brennan, Alexandra Bernetich, Emily Broadwell, Peter kempson, Megan Suau, Katie Jenkins, Nicole Keroack, Abbey Ness

light well

urban garden

green tech

high density housing

farmer's market

artists' lofts

Section Perspective

trains

the Pavilion

light well

high density houseing

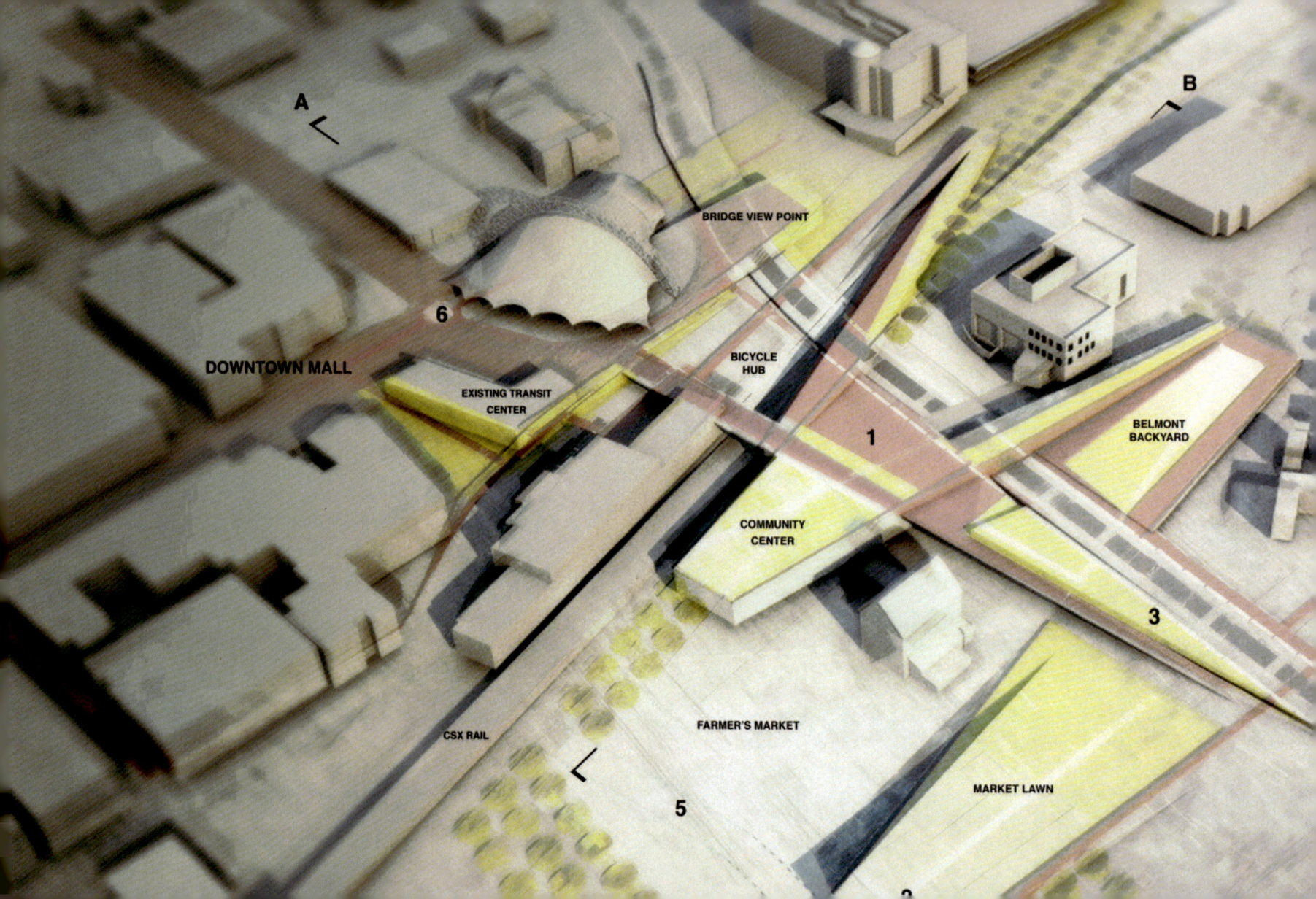

A

B

BRIDGE VIEW POINT

6

DOWNTOWN MALL

EXISTING TRANSIT
CENTER

BICYCLE
HUB

1

BELMONT
BACKYARD

COMMUNITY
CENTER

3

CSX RAIL

FARMER'S MARKET

5

MARKET LAWN

BELMONT

4

CHARLOTTESVILLE GATEWAYS

Our proposal is a series of "gateways" that stretch the bridge formally, conceptually, and performatively. The gateways choreograph the intersection of multiple modes of traffic, multiple programs, and multiple publics, generating a unique public space that marks the threshold to downtown.

The Belmont Bridge area is a site of intersections between the city's major traffic corridors, its neighborhoods, and the Downtown Mall. As a gesture of urban renewal, the existing bridge is an infrastructure that privileges the automobile, inhibits pedestrian and bicycle access, and forms divisive edges between the site's adjacent neighborhoods.

Our proposal negotiates, structures, and imaginatively juxtaposes these corridors and edges through series of gateways that 'break' and 're-stitch' this condition. Circulation is diversified and connections between downtown Charlottesville the neighborhoods south of the Mall are

enhanced. The proposed gates are sectionally programmatic and form an urban infrastructure for the city's farmer's market and a proposed bicycle hub. These programs uniquely define Charlottesville within broader economic and ecological networks. The farmers and cyclists that temporarily appropriate these spaces connect city's local residents and year-round visitors, at the bridge site, with adjacent communities and counties.

Earthwork from the 1905 and 1961 bridges is preserved. The topographic palimpsest of connections that were made and lost at the site become armatures, anchoring the design's gateways. The earthwork that forms a barrier at the Mall's eastern edge is transformed into an elevated park, creating a moment of prospect that situates the site within its regional context through views to the surrounding Piedmont Mountains and local landmarks.

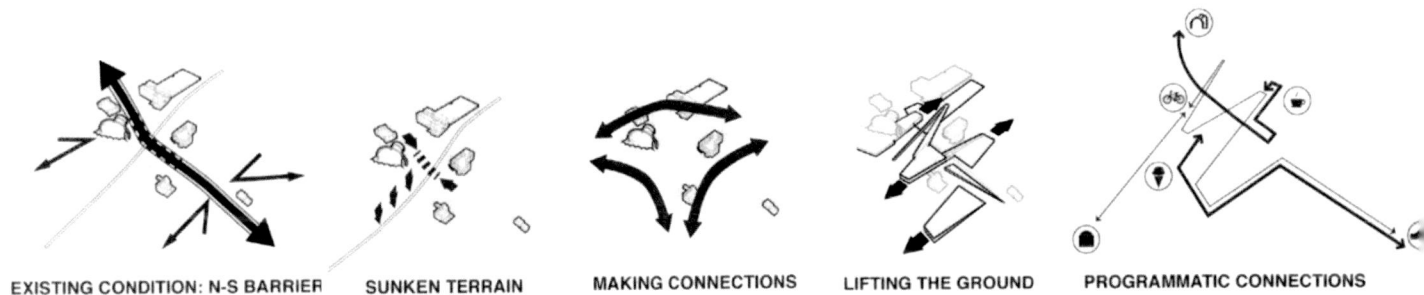

EXISTING CONDITION: N-S BARRIER   SUNKEN TERRAIN   MAKING CONNECTIONS   LIFTING THE GROUND   PROGRAMMATIC CONNECTIONS

ADVISOR: Zaneta Hong; TEAM: Emily kathryn Ashby, Ephraim Ryan Chaney, Michael Taylor Herring, Rebecca Hightower, Jessica Julia Hays, Joseph Lloyd, Patrick Mayfield, Danielle Alexander, Teppei Iizuka, Daniel Mowery, Jen Lynch

PAVILION   MARKET STREET   BIKE HUB   CSX RAIL   COMMUNITY CENTER   BELMONT BACKYARD

Gateways allow for sectional programs within cantilevered platforms.

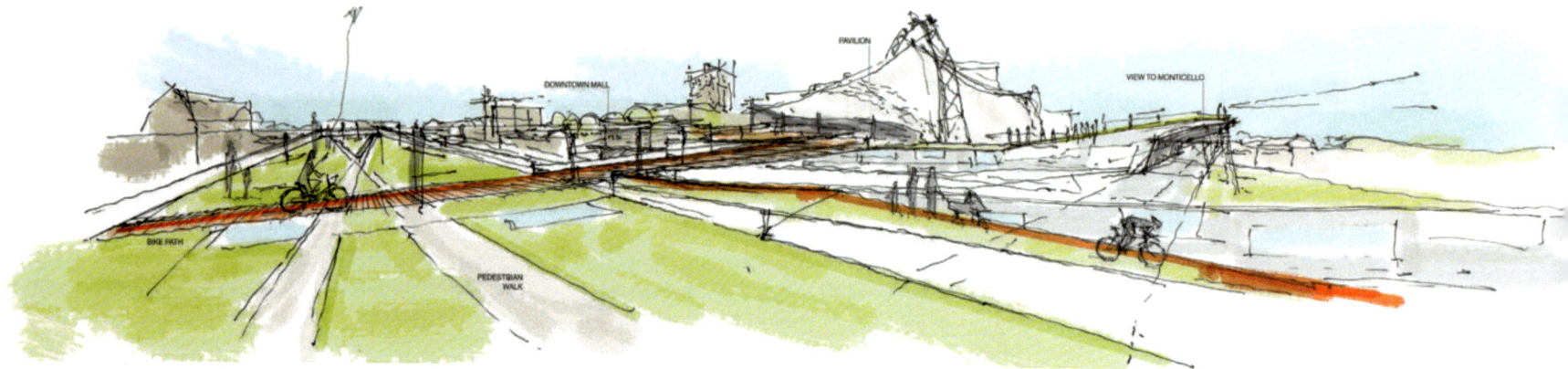

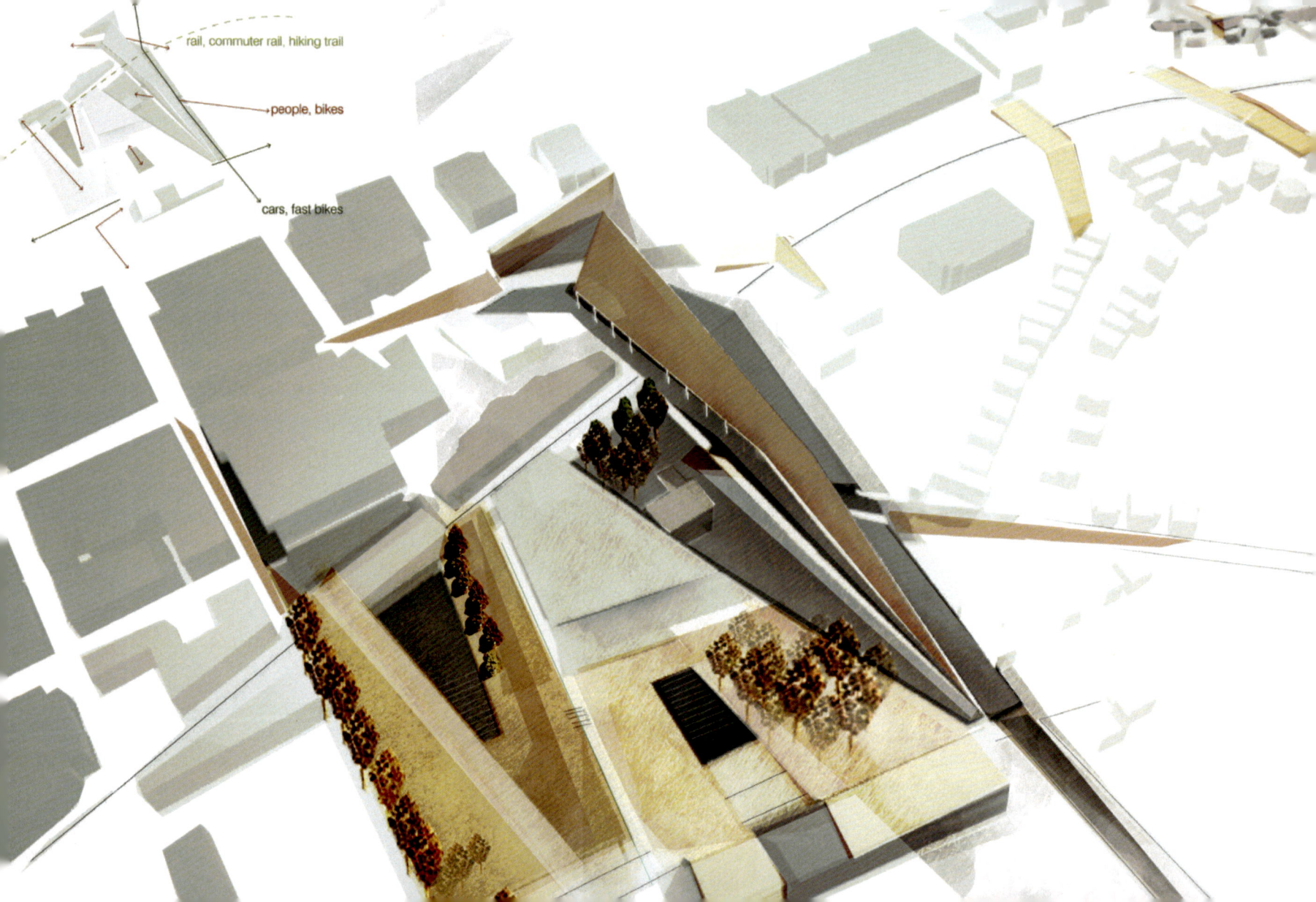

rail, commuter rail, hiking trail

people, bikes

cars, fast bikes

ONCE UPON A TIME

Our scheme creates multiple connections across Charlottesville's railroad tracks as a way to connect various adjoining neighborhoods in the city. Currently, both physical and implied boundaries exist between Belmont, North Downtown and the Garrett Street area. One such boundary is the CSX operated railroad tracks that pass straight through the area. Our proposal stitches together pedestrian paths across the length of the tracks where informal routes currently exist.

Near the footprint of the current Belmont Bridge, our proposal consists of a series of tilted planes that enclose an indoor/outdoor farmers' market complex, a new amphitheater, restaurants, and work/live space. The tilted planes also separate pedestrian and bike traffic from automobile traffic providing a safe, comfortable pedestrian route that is uninterrupted during local events. Most importantly, this area also serves as a new ending to the mall, an open democratic park space that the downtown area currently lacks.

New buildings to the north and south of this new Belmont Bridge serve as bookends to our proposed redevelopment. A large building at Garrett and Avon encloses our new park space and provides numerous mixed use and mixed income units. Another building at Market and Ninth serves as a new visitors' center, centrally located at the end of the new automobile portion of the bridge.

Work live units are carved into the hillside in the previously underdeveloped area farther east along the railroad tracks. In the same area, a series of smaller bridges connect Belmont with this area north of the tracks and the new work live units. These smaller bridges are large enough to accommodate future program, such as restaurants or outdoor lounging areas. The bridges not only serve current area inhabitants but also will be utilized by residents of planned further developments along this section of the tracks.

ADVISOR: Alexander Kitchin; TEAM: Soo kyung Lee, Sydna Winfree Mundy, Han Jin, Yetunde Ogunwumi, Whitney Paul, E. Burgess Rice, Taylor Scott, Xin Zhong, Liz Kneller, Whitney Newton, Nathan Burgess

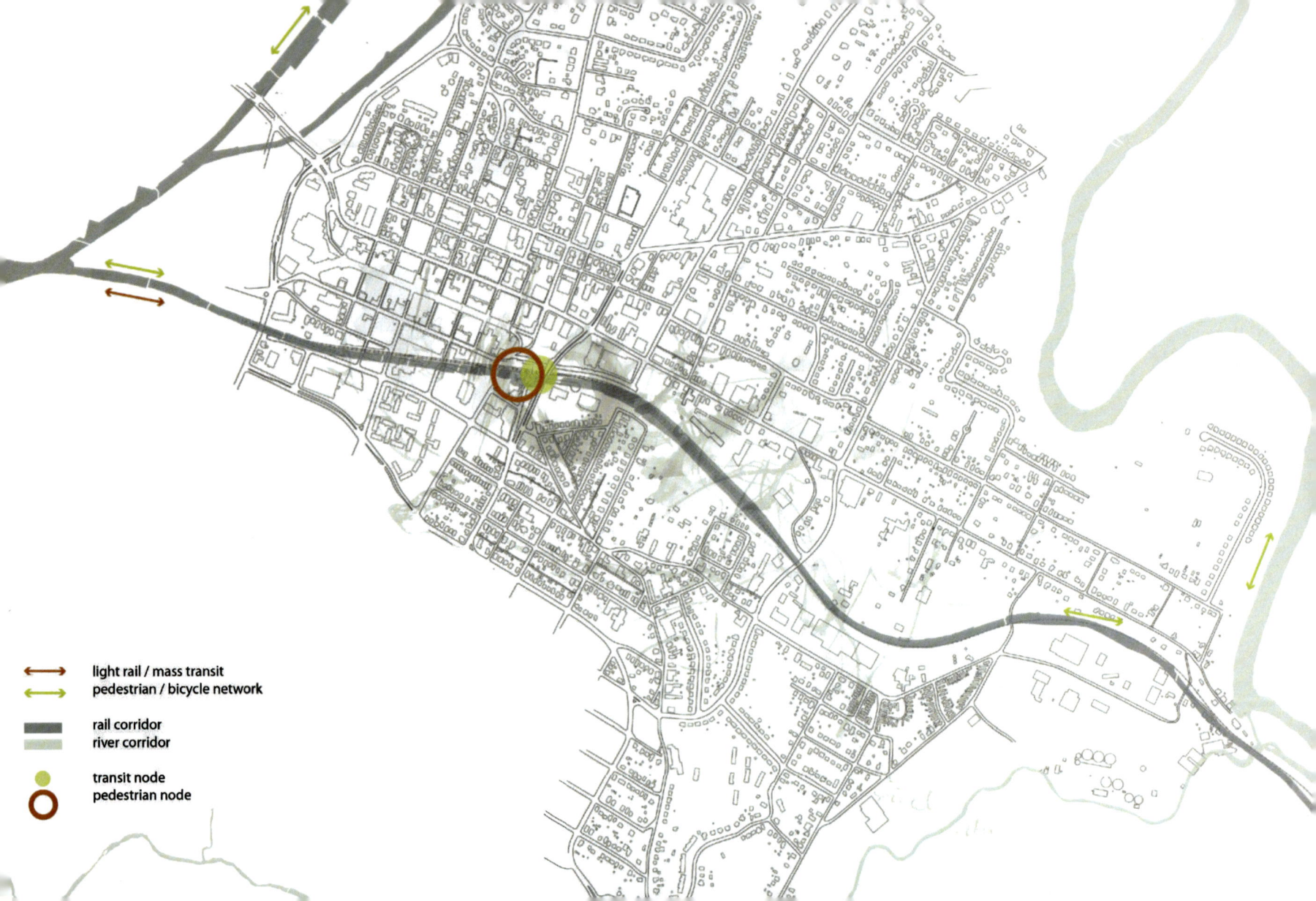

light rail / mass transit
pedestrian / bicycle network

rail corridor
river corridor

transit node
pedestrian node

WALK THE LINES

At the heart of Charlottesville, the Belmont Bridge shapes part of a mighty knot. It absorbs a network of connections which reach beyond Downtown and Belmont to all the communities of Charlottesville, Albemarle County, across the Piedmont and beyond.

The current 1961 bridge, while allowing traffic to cross the railroad tracks, restricts contact between many of these populations. Walk the Lines envisions a meeting place at this crucial juncture. By providing a platform for connectivity, we envision a future hub for transit, contact, passage and leisure at all speeds and scales. Pedestrians, cyclists, commuters and visitors all find paths to move and places to pause.

The platform structure spans the railroad beneath the road bridge, reaching out to the surrounding neighborhoods while simultaneously enveloping semi-enclosed spaces that provide a variety of areas for different programs and activity.

A landscaped path beneath a trellised canopy leads from Belmont to a new City Market at the foot of the original 1905 bridge abutment. A permanent produce market in the old mill building brings year-round grocery shopping to the underserved Belmont area. From the platform above the tracks, ramps reach down to the transit center, the amphitheater, and a new play park east of 9th Street. The solid canopy over the stage of the re-graded amphitheater allows lawn seating facing west along the downtown mall toward the Blue Ridge Mountains, providing much-needed public seating for the mall. Automobile traffic continues largely in its current pattern, while pressure on the bridge intersections is relieved by a new grade crossing at Goodman/10th Streets. Reducing the currently underused four traffic lanes to two (plus bike lanes) allows for construction of the parallel bridge-park. This juncture will become a crucial component of the city's future growth, allowing future phases of development to take place without disrupting neighborhood life.

ADVISOR: Karolin Moellman; TEAM: Alexander M. Picciano, Ximena Robelo Gutierrez, Anfal Elnour Adam , Kaitlyn Anne Badlato, Stephanie Burcham, Joseph Huennekens, Alan Ford, Harsh Jain, Jake Fox, Leah Wener, Doug Dickerson

B

C

D

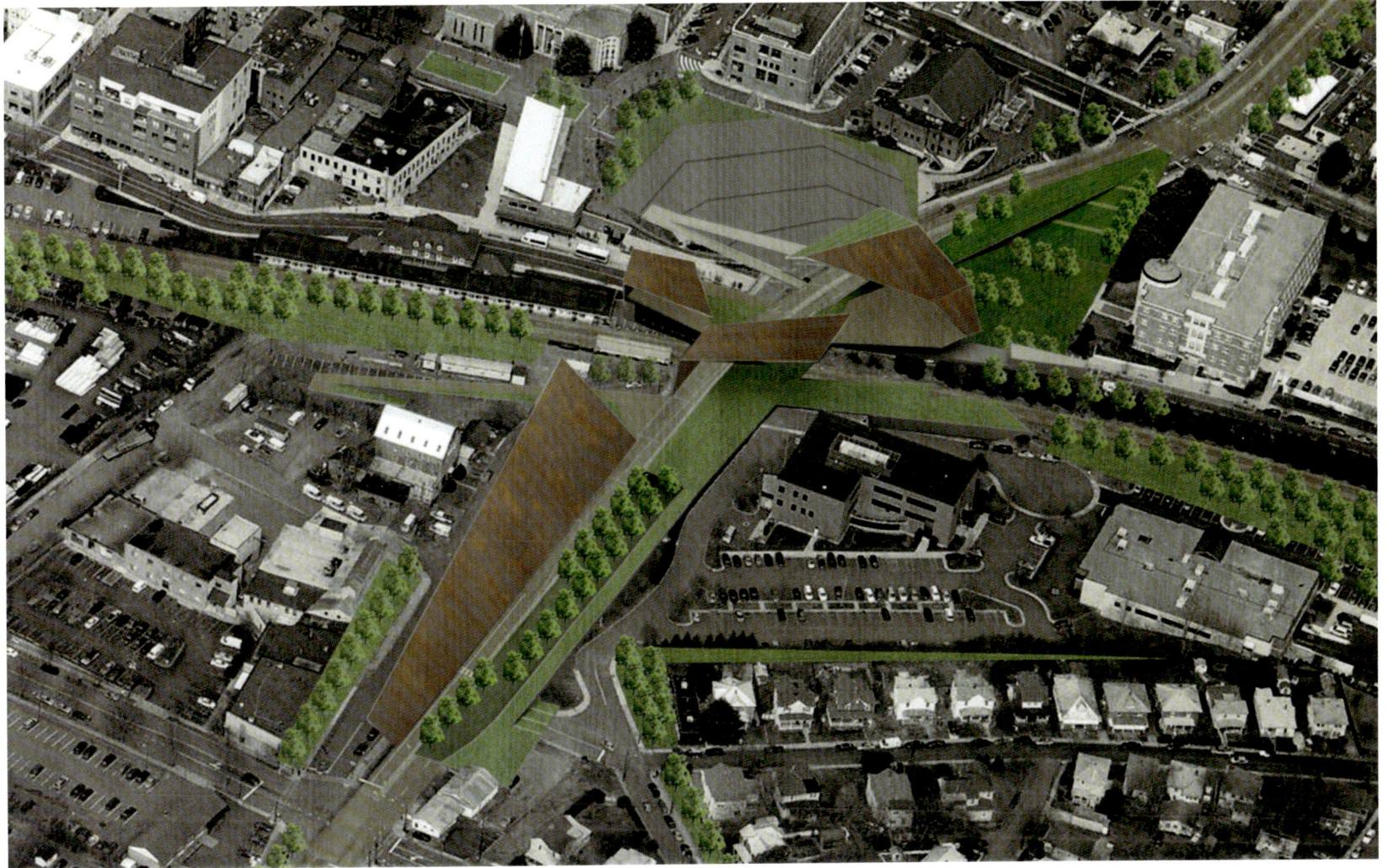

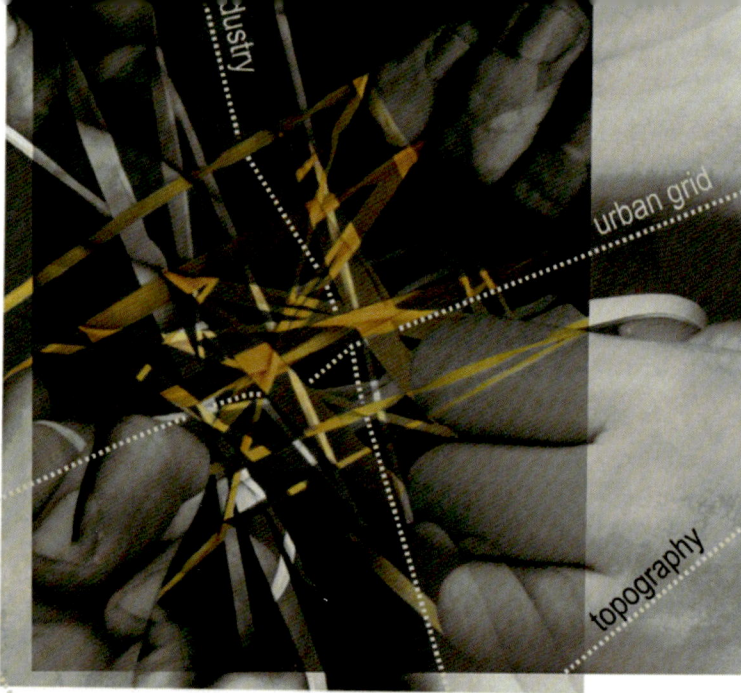

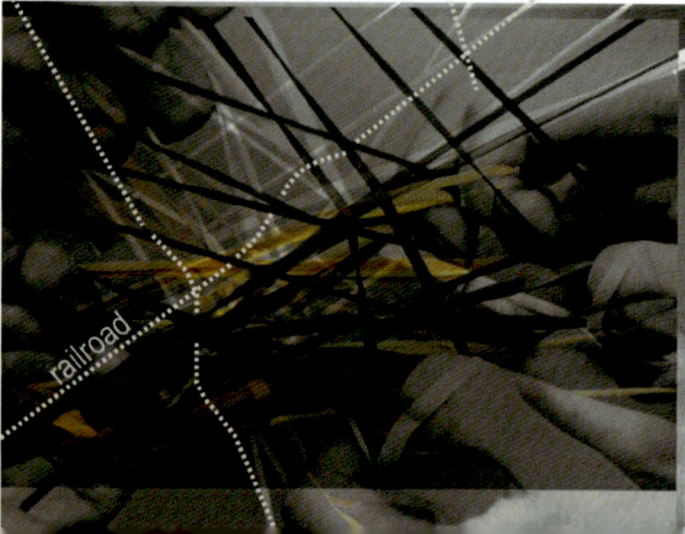
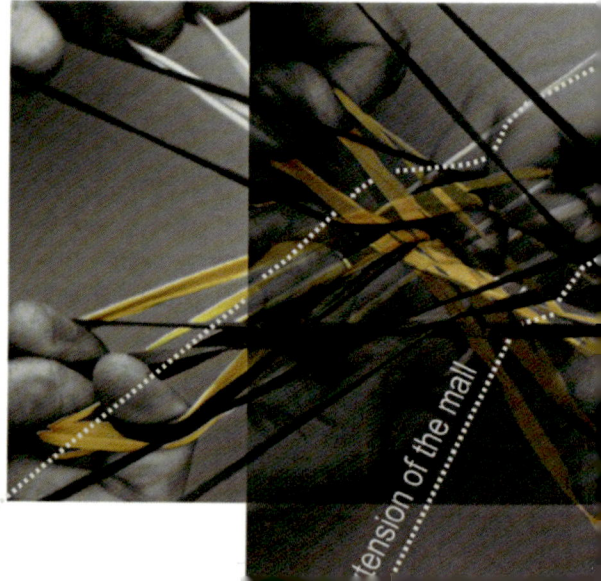

dustry

urban grid

topography

vehicular traffic

railroad

tension of the mall

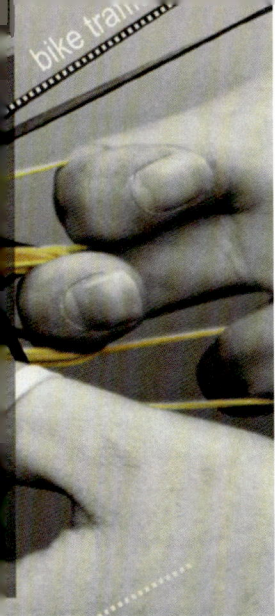

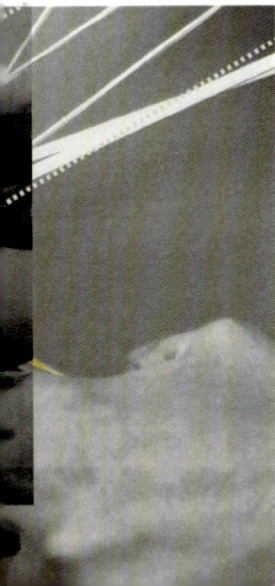

THE SQUISHY JOINT

This is a Node, a Catalyst—the SQUISHY JOINT at which void becomes vortex. Shaped by forces both internal and external, strands emerge from the urban landscape and interact to form connections between neighborhoods and rooms—spaces to meander, meditate, and be surrounded by the vitality of the city, rather than to simply traverse.

The lifeless bypass becomes a system of continuity and controlled chaos, with layers of movement and the addition of landscape giving rise to scenic views, unique soundscapes and moments of profound sensorial experience. The Gateway provides a point of convergence, the Spoke weaves and redirects, and the Crow's Nest overlooks the choreography and composition of downtown while framing views of the nearby mountains. Dogwoods welcome visitors at entry points, while grasses planted in a linear fashion inhabit narrow passageways. Vines climb the structure at nodes to offer respite and vibrant color. The form places you in the canopy of sycamores, while ferns and viburnum flourish in the resulting shade. Finally, the space between the lattices becomes the Orchard and the Beech, a forest and farmer's market where the community can gather in the shade of a grove permeated by historic buildings, railways, and the music of the urban and planted environments.

From this node there will emerge a new focus on connectivity and transportation, encouraging reactions to solve existing disconnects in biking and pedestrian infrastructure as well as to create a more functional and sustainable transit network for the city. Molded by the city itself, the SQUISHY JOINT offers an adaptive, tri-modal transportation structure that connects the Downtown Pedestrian Mall to the surrounding neighborhoods and beyond, while creating a promenade of choreographed interaction and sensory experience as well as a new community commons that serves to invigorate a historic hub of transportation, industry, and cultural activity for the city of Charlottesville.

ADVISOR: Anselmo Canfora; TEAM: Danussa Vejar , Austin Reid Walker, Taylor Nicole Baskin, Annesley Grace Berndt, Yi Li, Patrick Schoonover, Lain Jaing, Quifan Wu , Jesse Wilks , Erin Root

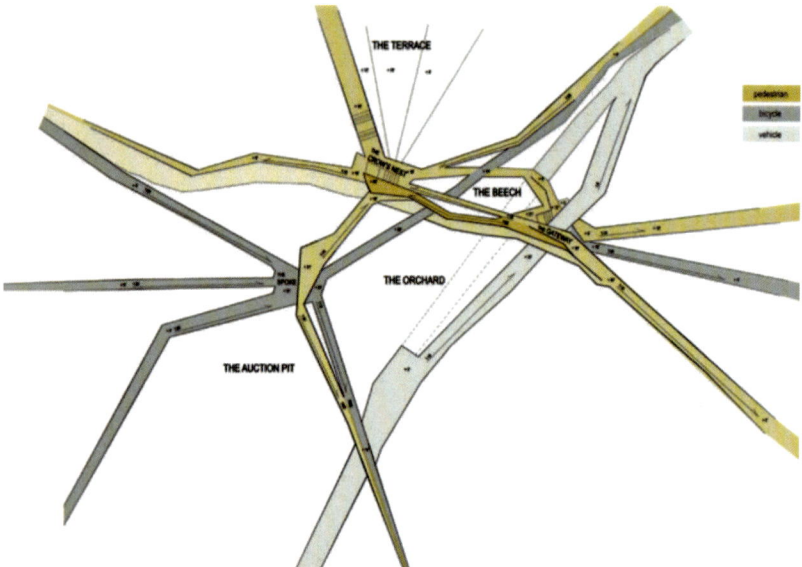

THE TERRACE

THE BEECH

THE ORCHARD

THE AUCTION PIT

pedestrian
bicycle
vehicle

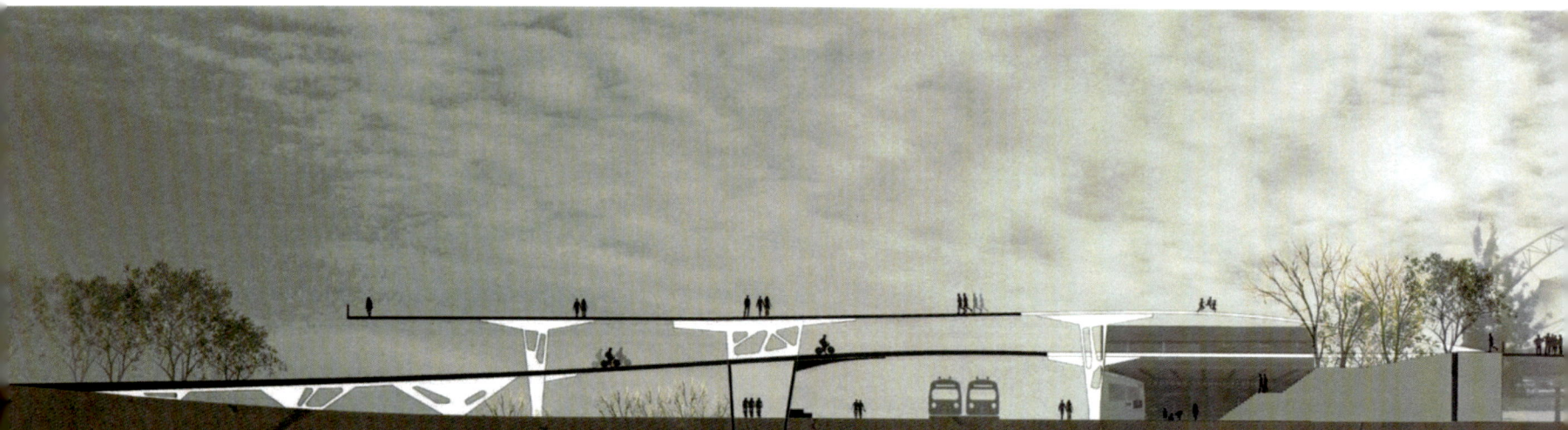

CVILLACTIVE SURFACE

C'villActive Surface is a multi-storied, thick surface that behaves as both landscape and architecture. This active surface is composed of public spaces that connect a variety of developments—including residential housing, permanent space for the Charlottesville Farmers Market, offices for technology research, and community studios for industrial design and manufacturing. It integrates the transit center with the historic train station as a new hub for both public transport and food distribution.

The surface connects the existing neighborhoods of Downtown, Belmont and Ridge Street through a system of pedestrian ramps that slope up to cross the train tracks and thicken to provide conditioned spaces for developments. In section, the structure creates three distinct spaces: a ground level providing at grade railroad crossings for pedestrians and cyclists, a thick middle zone that contains conditioned programs such as offices and housing, and a top level that acts as a public park space.

Vehicles cross the surface along a two lane road that ramps up through the park to touch down on the north side of the Downtown Mall. Food carts populate certain areas of the upper platform, activating temporary public spaces.

C'villActive Surface branches out along the railroad corridor, extending into a bike path that connects downtown to the east side of Belmont at Beer Run Restaurant, and then further through to the Rivanna park. The new gesture along the railroad extends the Mall across the tracks— culminating in a new downtown Pavilion that performs not only as a point of arrival, but also as a threshold to Charlottesville's diverse neighborhoods.

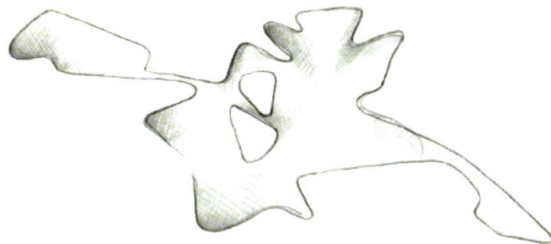

upper canopy

RESIDENTIAL
COMMERCIAL
RESTAURANTS
MARKET
PAVILION

programs

ADVISORS: Inaki Alday, Beth Meyer; TEAM: William Durburrow Munford, Marcy Nicole Wheeler, Seth William Brown, Sarah Anne Buchholz, Tracie Jordan Cabler, Sarah Scott, Xiao Wu, Sarah Cancienne , Judy Chang, Chris Woods , Elizabeth Russell

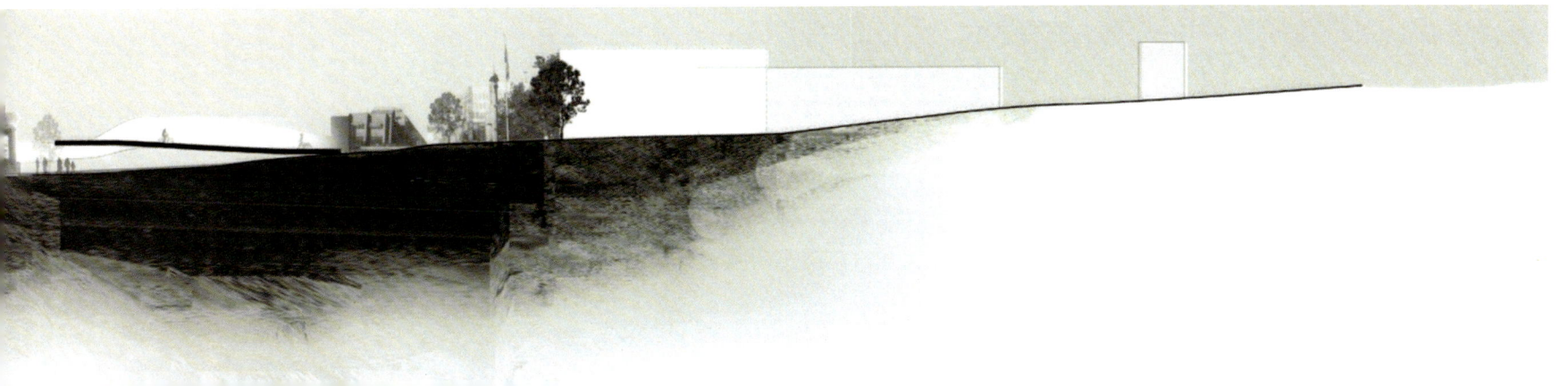

X-ING

At the meeting place now referred to as the 'Belmont Bridge,' there are two bypasses: road and rail. The implicit imperatives of these two infrastructures have done more to organize the urban fabric of Charlottesville over the last century and a half than any of the city's planners, presidents, or politicians. This project proposes that the city cease to be organized by its infrastructure, and instead begin to organize the infrastructure.

X-ING proposes that the so called 'Belmont Bridge' be understood as an organizational infrastructure, within which the city's most underserved desires intertwine with the cities most over-served imperatives. All that is required is choreography. The trains must never stop running. Coal trains, garden trains, swimming pool trains, trains for the washing and wagging of dogs, trains for impromptu parties, disco, nomadic art exhibitions and temporary housing. The more trains the better: each an autonomous island, in an organizational matrix. Train schedules will be coordinated from the 'Belmont Bridge,' itself a transportation hub for railroad passengers switching to and from buses and cars.

The same strategy applied to the rail lines will be applied to the bridge traffic. In-between peak times, the surface of the bridge will be reduced to one lane in either direction, appropriating this space for bike, pedestrians, and formal balls. During peak times, the surface of the terminal itself will be used for crossing.

Finally, X-ING proposes to increase the amount of rail lines to its former levels in the 1940's. This calls for a supply of wood for railroad-ties. Since X-ING is proposing that rail lines be used as concert space, it now proposes to re-imagine the NTelos Pavilion as the largest tree planter on the downtown mall, capable of supporting a tree nursery, which will function as a publically accessible forest.

ADVISORS: Tat Bohnevi, Beth Meyer; TEAM: Saman Zomorodi, Megan Jane Carpenter, Mark Elliott Curry , Ethan Wayne Ford, George Daniel klett, Reni Young, Ahmad Darab, Alex D'Aversa , Cooper Jones, Rebekah Dye, Seth Denizen

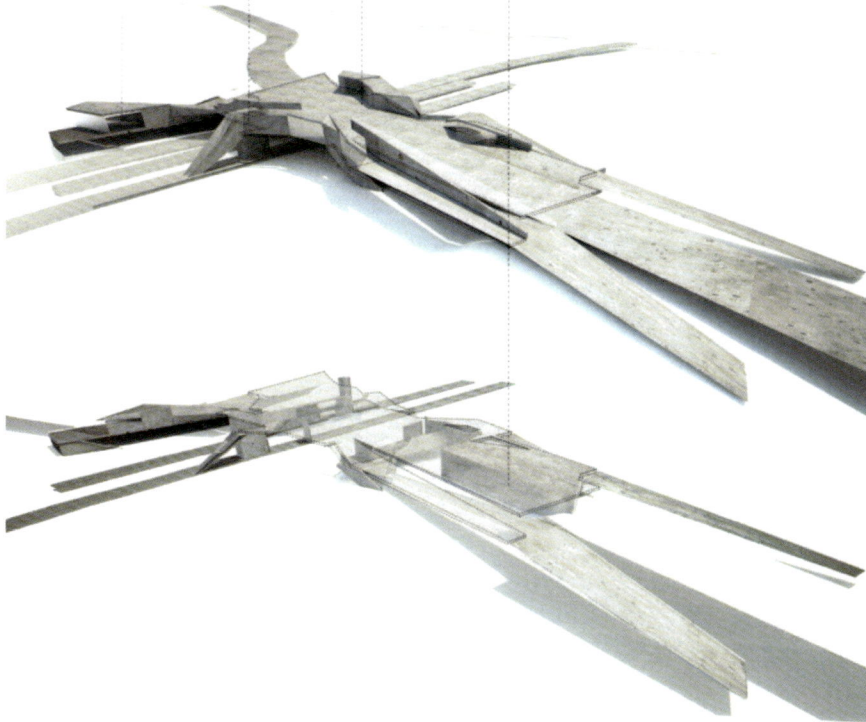

Ticketing Office

Access to Platforms

Greyhound + Starlight
Bus Station

WEAVE BRIDGE

The Weave Bridge Project seeks to remediate the erosion of our public space by imagining a new bridge as a landscape, city park, market, and urban center– creating an urban destination that reunites Belmont and downtown Charlottesville.   The bridge creates a public park as a destination above vehicular traffic that visually connects Charlottesville to the surrounding cultural and natural landscape. It touches the ground in new places to provide improved pathways for human accessibility while the bend in the roadway intentionally slows vehicles to 15 MPH in order to enhance the experience and safety of the pedestrian. The structure integrates the sloping ground-plane to create active, public landscapes through a wide array of flexible open spaces. Specifically, new locations are created for the Farmer's Market, the rebirth of the Belmont Market as grassroots music venue, a community bicycle shop, skate-park and public art and theater opportunities.

Through the analysis of the existing, fragmented grid, the project proposes a new urban lattice not based on vehicles or industry, but grounded in broader notions of social accessibility, freedom of speech, and our common cultural foundation as citizens of Charlottesville. Conceptually, four new guidelines are the threads that weave a re-envisioned grid: (1) the path from Friendship Court to the base of the 1905 Belmont Bridge; (2) the historic Monticello Road from downtown Belmont to the downtown Mall; (3) the line that connects the trajectory of the Graffiti Wall to the Freedom of Speech Monument (4) the city spine of the Mall with the Freedom of Speech Monument at its heart.

From this geometric framework, derived from these existing socio-physical threads, the Weave Bridge emerges as the connection, icon, and embodiment of a better gateway for a new Charlottesville.

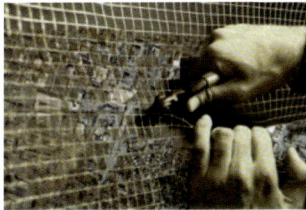

integrated weave diagram

free speech diagram

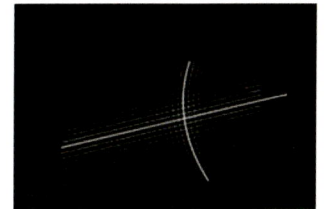

social accessibility diagram

ADVISORS: Schaeffer Somers; TEAM: Katherine Parrish Brandy, Arisa Chentaphun, Joshua Aries J Cruz, Maximilian Brenner, Christopher Chu, Regina Davis, Katherine Filipour, Asa Rector Eslocker, Shiguang Chen, Margaret Sydnor, Lingyi Gu

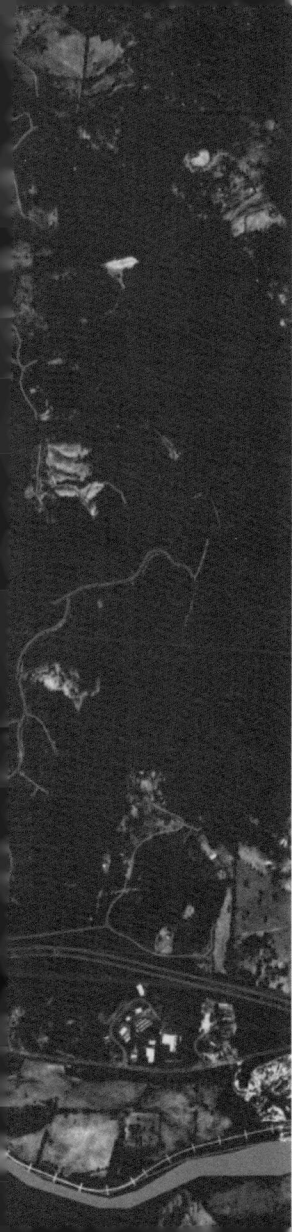

MULTI-MODAL NEXUS

The Belmont Bridge in its existing state fails to enhance the larger alternative transportation networks in Charlottesville, or strengthen potential relationships between surrounding neighborhoods. The current design of the bridge lacks connectivity because pedestrians are treated as an afterthought to vehicular traffic. Coupled with the East/West boundary formed by the railroad, pedestrians are left with only one option, the small sidewalk on one side of the bridge. Our design emerged from mapping multiple networks in Charlottesville, including parks, bike and trails, and public transportation routes. We sought to enhance and re-imagine how neighborhoods that are divided by infrastructure like the railroad—could be stitched back together. Therefore we wanted our design to tie into existing networks and strengthen weak links. We saw this connectivity happening in three dimensions, both on elevated spaces and on the ground beaneath. The form of the bridge extends the Downtown Mall, permeates existing boundaries and creates multiple destinations with calculated views of the regional landscape. These views offer moments for contemplating our place within a larger region and perhaps allow us to reflect on the history and transformations of the land. A collection of new paths, roads and gathering spaces serving pedestrians, cyclists and motorists push the possibilities of how a bridge can perform in our city. Our bridge design is a network consisting of two main components: skeleton and skin. While the skeleton structures a formal hierarchy of public spaces for gathering and multiple modes of transportation, the skin adapts as it moves through space. Becoming both an awning and a walk-able surface—a 2nd level of connectivity is formed creating spatial fluidity. In order to extend downtown into Belmont the pavilion was relocated and reinterpreted. The new amphitheatre is situated on the opposite side of the railroad where it will no longer serve as a hard boundary to the east end of the mall. An open square, ideal for weekend farmers markets and temporary vendors, will occupy the pavilion's former site. This program spills onto the elevated spaces into Belmont during the busy summer months. The new market space will strengthen the connections between surrounding neighborhoods and provide much needed access to fresh food. This location allows the market to network with local communities, vendors and merchants. With its form, contextual position and strategic program, our design goes beyond spanning the railroad. It creates a new and needed network that strengthens the existing local and regional connections.

ADVISOR: Mara Marcu; TEAM: Arliss Lane Gearhart, Karleen Ashley Fajardo, Phoebe Harris, Isaac Min kim, Sarah Kohlhepp, Rebecca Lewis, Marcus Brooks, Yeonkyung Oh, Aaron Gahr, Aja Bulla-Richards, Regina Pencile

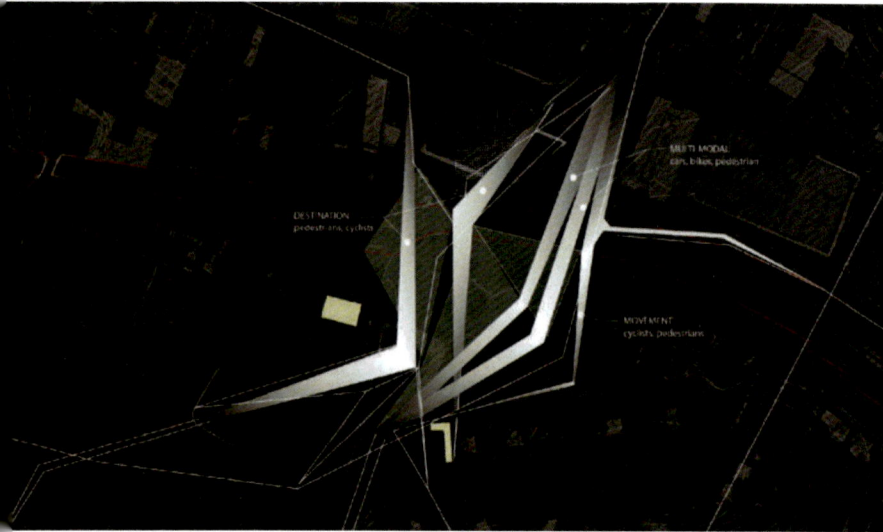

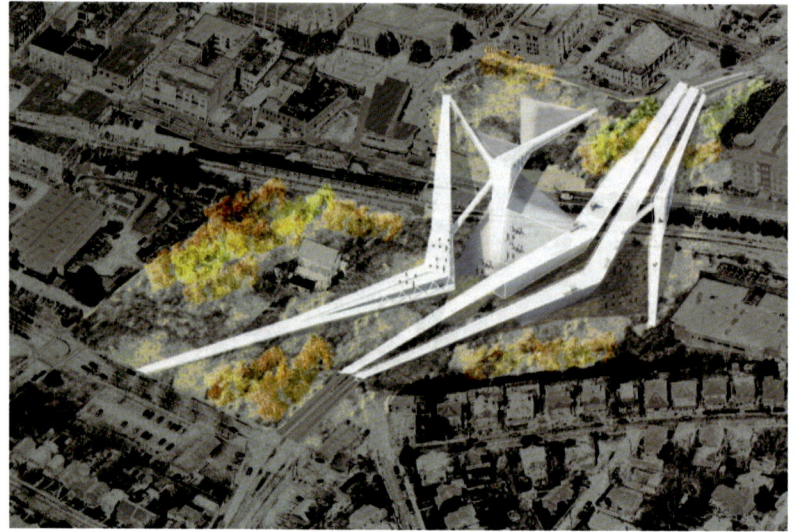

PATH PROGRAMS PLACE

This design for the Belmont Bridge reconnects the physically divided community of Belmont with the Downtown Mall by proposing a strong, geometric language that emphasizes pedestrian flows across and through this threshold site. In addition to moving people and vehicles, the flowing paths define new places on both sides of the tracks and create programmed space that will reinvigorate the Belmont Bridge area. The space beneath the new iconic pedestrian bridge and vehicular bridge will be transformed into the permanent home for the Charlottesville Farmer's Market. The edges of this space are defined by the ramping pedestrian bridge, which also provides cover for vendors. Other edge areas will be converted into public spaces, including a corridor for potential new development.

These geometric moves and gestures emphasize the pedestrian experience. At the apex of the bridge, the individual rises above the traffic to capture views of Monticello. Traffic lanes will be reduced to one lane each way, providing a wider pedestrian sidewalk and dedicated bike lanes. On-grade paths connect from both the Transit Station and the Pavilion to the Belmont Neighborhoods. The new Belmont Bridge will provide access to the vast amenities that Charlottesville has to offer while creating new exciting places that will be attractions to both locals and visitors.

ADVISOR: Elizabeth Roettge; TEAM: Henry Luke Gates, Carolina Gutierrez Lacayo, Allen Merced-Figueroa, Tae Joon Park, Phillip Hoover Redpath, Annie Locke Scherer, Silvi Stefi, Eric Wong, Nick Wickersham, Kate Hayes, Jasmine Amanin

THE CITY BRIDGE

The restructuring of the link between Belmont & Downtown offers an opportunity to increase economic development and social cohesion in Charlottesville. Currently, the Belmont Bridge produces a tremendous amount of underutilized space beneath it and acts as an underwhelming conclusion to Charlottesville's urban jewel, the Downtown Mall. Using the bridge as a formal and economic catalyst, the design generates development and connections over and around the tracks as well as extending the pedestrian-scale of the Mall along the tracks to the east.

The design proposes a two-bridge suspension system, safely separating vehicle traffic from pedestrians and cyclists. While the vehicle bridge uses the same launching points as the current bridge, the pedestrian bridge offers a direct connection between Belmont and Friendship Court with the public transit station on the Mall. Earthen mounds

shaped from the current bridge abutments as well as the bridge itself give form to a flexible park that can accommodate many uses at once-- farmer's markets, performance space, playgrounds and more. Replacing the semi-private Pavilion, this public space serves to anchor the Mall with the proposed mixed use development along and extended Water Street.

New buildings built beneath the southern end of the bridge make this a major entry point to Downtown. Housing car parking as well as bike sharing and repair facilities, visitors are encouraged to park and cycle to Downtown even before crossing the bridge in their car. By establishing new routes of multi-modal circulation, people and places are brought closer together, creating new physical and social connections.

ADVISORS: Karen Van Lengen, Craig Barton; TEAM: Brianna Nicole Thompson, Megan Elizabeth Watson, Jia Hu, Carlos Elliott Jennings, Kelsey Vitullo , Weishun Xu, Samantha Saunders, Tina Cheng, Ryan Metcalf, Pete Malandra, Michael Britt

BELMONT EXCHANGE

The Belmont Exchange focuses on highlighting the pedestrian experience. This comes in many forms, such as utilizing local and regional resources, catering to multi-income communities, and enhancing the pre-existing local experiences. As a whole, the Belmont Exchange provides a link between the Downtown and Belmont communities by turning the Belmont Bridge into a location rather than a point of passing. Using the community issues brought forth by the citizens of Belmont as a guide, the creation of a pedestrian path was a key component in the design process. The Belmont Exchange builds off the original structure of the bridge, limiting the auto traffic to two lanes and creating a boardwalk for pedestrians to safely enjoy local food and views of the mountains. Charlottesville, a hub of the local food movement, has been in search of a permanent home for its City Market. The Exchange expands the idea of the

bridge, creating a plaza and boardwalk made of local materials and offering a new location for the market. Using food carts and tables along the walkway gives communities on both sides of the Bridge and beyond an easily accessible site on which to sell and purchase local foods. In the future, we propose that the market will grow, encompassing the lower Belmont side of the Bridge and expanding into vacant space. Lastly, this project proposes the development of a concrete industry focused on the Belmont side of the bridge, resourced by sand dredged in Norfolk and brought by currently existing rail lines. This sand would not only be a resource to this industry, but would also serve as a recreational space when not being used for production. The concrete produced would provide raw material for further growth in the Belmont "downtown" area.

year 1

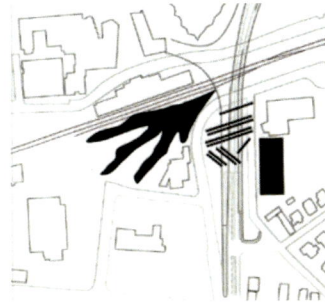

year 3

year 5

year 10

ADVISORS: Kristina Hill, Craig Barton; TEAM: Laura Emma Lee, Paola Cecilia Mayorga, John Anthony Perona, Emily Rebecca Scott, Jacob Thomas Tuzzo, kyle Bancroft, Jamie Dean, You Li, Michael Goddard, Michael Geffel, Brian Davis

THE GRID, THE FLOUR MILL & THE LANDSCAPE LINE

Our proposal—The Grid, The Flour Mill and The Landscape Line—draws on Charlottesville's rich urban history and radical choice of walkability as exemplified by Lawrence Halprin's Pedestrian Mall. These three forms act as the instigators of a new urban center and market plaza that expand the pedestrian realm and connects the Downtown core to the neighborhoods south of the C&O Railroad tracks. The Downtown grid and the Belmont neighborhood grid meet to create a new, at-grade road which acts as primary vehicular gateway to Downtown replacing the perceived need for the current Belmont Bridge. Once again we make the radical choice of walkability proposing to retrace the alignment of the historic bridge over the tracks as a new pedestrian and bicycle connection that extends Monticello Road uniting Belmont's existing neighborhood center to the Mall's East End plaza and amphitheater. At the intersection of the new pedestrian bridge and the Landscape Line is a new urban plaza around the historic Brown Milling Co. Flour

Mill. The Flour Mill becomes a central icon along the diagonal axis of the Landscape Line. The Line, a diagonal axis, unites emerging development areas stretching from the Frank IX parcel to the south, through the Flour Mill, and terminating at the Martha Jefferson Development parcel. The Landscape Line creates a linear park which mirrors the strength of Halprin's Downtown Mall and reconnects the Mill site to the neighborhood of Friendship Court and establishes a strong recreational amenity. Our vision is of a mixed income, mixed use neighborhood of city blocks, 3-6 stories high, animated by ground floor neighborhood retail and farmer's market activities. This establishes an urban place centered on the Flour Mill and able to receive an interior location for a new farmer's market building. The Grid, The Flour Mill and The Landscape Line together transform the area into a new urban expression of Charlottesville's future.

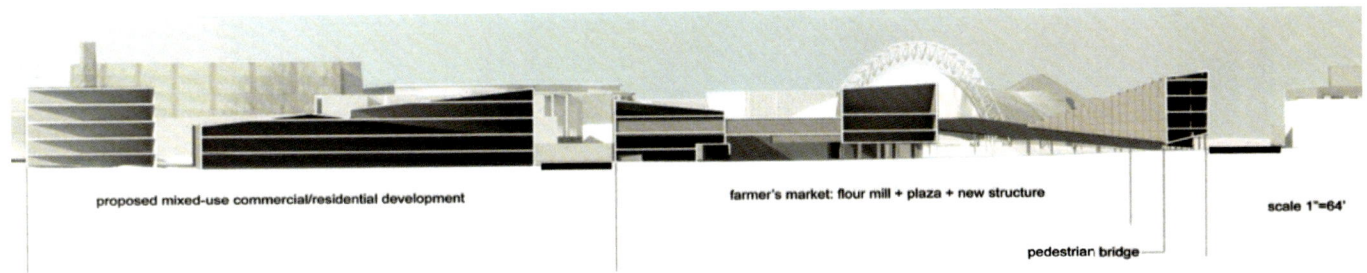

proposed mixed-use commercial/residential development

farmer's market: flour mill + plaza + new structure

pedestrian bridge

scale 1"=64'

ADVISORS: Maurice Cox, Daniel Bluestone; TEAM: Mikhail Maclaine Payson, Irene Preciado Arango, Evan Shepherd Burch, Laura Jean Burden, Eduardo Diaz-Etchevehere , Eric Hanna, Brianne Doak, Ryan Lewandowski, Luhan Zhou, Silas Haslam

BELLIVILLE // CONNECTING THE CITY & THE GRITTY

Charlottesville is a city of diverse neighborhoods, each with their own character. Belmont is strikingly different from the tree-enclosed spaces of the downtown mall. Currently, Charlottesville's pedestrian mall ends suddenly at 9th Avenue, with four lanes of traffic and an intimidating expanse of asphalt. Our project aims to connect downtown Charlottesville to Belmont while preserving the unique character of the train yard, a rare moment of gritty industrial history. We propose to celebrate the grittiness of the yards by converting the area under the new bridge to a skate park, making the area under the bridge a significant part of Charlottesville's spatial experience. We propose a bridge that will be a monumental object set in the field of the train yards, bracketed by two different neighborhoods. The masts mark their respective sides and the cables suspend the mass of the road, forming a light lattice between the two masts. The pedestrian paths on the bridge will be

translucent and filled with light. On either end, the pedestrian paths swell to become spaces to listen to concerts, watch the trains, or take in the fantastic views. We propose to narrow the traffic lanes of the bridge, shaping it for the future pedestrians of Charlottesville. The areas under the bridge are just as critical to the creation of great public spaces downtown. We propose installing storefronts for bars, galleries and workshops along Water Street creating an area under the bridge that is just as exciting as being on top. A new bike path will run along the easement between the Water Street sidewalk and the train tracks, creating a path of movement and a chance to watch the trains. By creating a memorable bridge and augmenting Water Street and the train yards beneath, we propose to create a better Charlottesville by enhancing the unique character of the city instead of erasing the differences between its neighborhoods.

Two opposing urban conditions create a collaged landscape - a neighborhood

A singular gesture, a shared icon, connects the two absolutes within the city.

Multiple ground level connections provide multiple points of connection between neighborhoods.

ADVISORS: Ed Ford, Peter O'Shea; TEAM: Roshni Ashok Mahtani, Michael Joseph Sions, Demitra Elena Skipper , Fung Siang Tan Tai , Danielle Eads, James Bresnahan, Faith Cerny , Lauren Begen , Sameer-A Rayyan , James Moore

HUG IT OUT CVILLE

The current bridge divides the city. A new one can bring it back together. In the spirit of embracing a new vision for the belmont bridge, we ask you to Hug It Out, C'ville!

The Downtown Mall and the Belmont neighborhoods are vibrant communities. Our bridge provides the space for them to converge, grow, and interact, both with each other and with nearby neighborhoods such as Friendship Court and Martha Jefferson. These connections can take place across a zone that includes a new physical bridge as well as a set of public spaces and revitalized streets that form a community strategy of bridging. We propose to create a

new neighborhood as part of this bridge, supported by a network of new public spaces that promote a spirit of activism and community engagement through public art, spaces that can be appropriated, and events that channel the unique energy of Charlottesville.

How to hug a city:

1. Take what's there
2. Embrace, connect and frame spaces
3. Catazlye public expression
4. Energize the city

ADVISORS: Nancy Takahashi, Peter O'Shea; TEAM: Anne Julia Tavetian, Ellison Blair Turpin, Jennifer Chi Fang, Alejandro Garrido Perez, Kerry Garikes, Ting Ting Jin, Clayton Williams, Jason Layel, Kara Lanahan, Alexa Bush, Rachel Nelson

BRIDGE OVER RUBBLED WATER

Bridge Over Rubbled Water repurposes the railway below the Belmont Bridge—a critical seam between Downtown Charlottesville and the Belmont Neighborhood—as a public greenway and connecting corridor. This strategy recycles and reconfigures artifacts of obsolete infrastructural growth—namely the existing bridge and the current underground storm water network. Additionally, it introduces an interactive system based on the optimal movement of water in the city, reversing the current hierarchy of human intervention over natural order. The design utilizes an analysis of the ideal geometry and flow of water in the city of Charlottesville—its collection, filtration, retention and movement—as if there were no artificial obstacles. From that, a proposal was conceived that

reinstitutes this geometry in the Downtown area, enabling the emergence of a healthier water network. The strategy recycles the rubble generated from the destruction of the current bridge, using it to form gabion walls that augment filtration, circulation and habitation, and significantly reduces the project's carbon footprint. Though designed for the specificity and particularity of the Belmont Bridge site, Bridge Over Rubbled Water could become a laboratory for testing emergent systems that reduce the burden of storm water on aging sewer systems, reveal water flows and processes to community members, mitigate contamination and erosion of area watersheds, and safely and effectively re-use post-industrial materials.

ADVISOR: Lucia Phinney; TEAM: Alexander Dean Kaplan, Samantha Lynn Weiser, Jamar Dimitri Moore, Timothy James O'Neill, Brittany Olivari, Kelly Pierson, Harriett A Jameson, Benjamin Sessa, Tom Gibbons, David Holzman, Catharine Killien

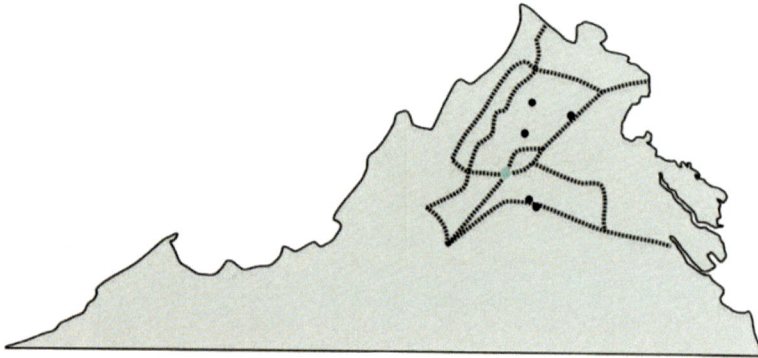

Demolition Waste Potential

■ = 10 gabion blocks

Existing
Belmont Bridge

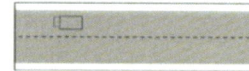

20,000 ft³ of demolition waste

=

190 gabion blocks

Current
Regional
Demolition
Projects

150,000 ft³ of demolition waste

=

1,500 gabion blocks

Capturing Stormwater Runoff

💧 = 1000 ft³ water

Existing
Belmont Bridge

38,000 ft³ impervious surface area

=

26,000 ft³ water runoff

Downtown
Pedestrian
Mall

670,000 ft³ impervious surface area

=

506,000 ft³ water runoff

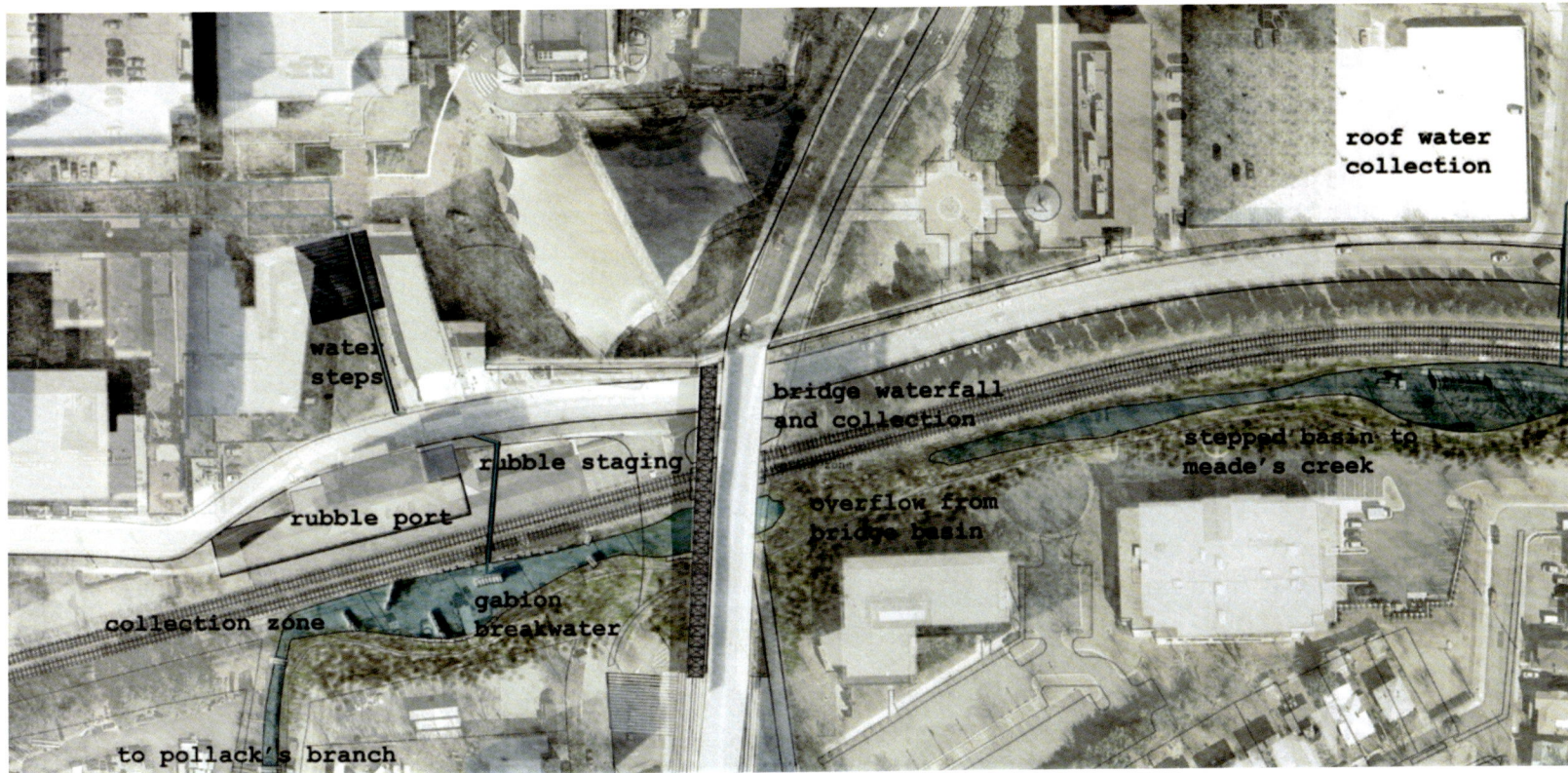

roof water
collection

water
steps

bridge waterfall
and collection

rubble staging

stepped basin to
meade's creek

rubble port

overflow from
bridge basin

collection zone

gabion
breakwater

to pollack's branch

ENGAGEMENT AND PROXIMITY

GATEWAY: Our proposal inhabits the space below the Belmont Bridge with pavilions that house stores and places to eat, as well as the City Market. It creates an intermediary connection to downtown Charlottesville and Belmont. The Mall extends across the tracks and links directly to Belmont with continuous activity.

FEASIBLE: It is not the physical location of the bridge that causes issues in connectivity, so existing structural columns are reused. The bridge can stay in use throughout construction since the bridge has two separate plates and traffic can be limited to one side of the deck.

MODAL: The Belmont Bridge is not simply about shuffling automobile traffic from one side of town to another. It presents an active point of overlap for pedestrians, bicycles, automobiles, and trains. The existing mall will be linked to Water Street and to Belmont in a more clear and definite way for pedestrians.

ICONIC: The form of the pedestrian bridge and pavilions have a quality of lightness and an expressed external structure building on the structural precedent of the Pavilion on the Mall. This lightness and articulation would contrast with the density of the existing concrete columns of the existing bridge.

GREEN: The layers of existing materials in the space between the bridge and the train tracks is retained. The ambiguous sense of place has directionality added to facilitate pedestrian movement across the tracks. Concrete pavers reflect the dimension of railroad ties and form regular patterns in active plaza spaces, becoming more scattered as spaces become less defined.

GATEWAY [Belmont and the Mall]
[Overlooked Ground]   FEASIBLE [less is more]   MODAL [Braided Activity]   ICONIC [Statement]   GREEN

ADVISOR: Julian Raxworthy; TEAM: Peiwei Zhang, Zachary Alexander Coles, Emma kimball Pierce, Cecilia Chase Camuzzi, Heather Medlin, Kelsey Reynolds, Gwendolyn Mcginn, Chris Brandt , Oscar Obando , Di Hu

CITY X-ING

City X-ing will be the new hub of transit and public life in Charlottesville. The space of the former Belmont Bridge becomes a multi-functional surface for transit, public space and diverse programs that enrich the city of Charlottesville and fold back into the existing urban fabric. The design enlivens the functional logistics of transit and circulation by integrating these flows into a series of new public spaces and programs. Motorists, cyclists and pedestrians share one surface, with one lane of automobile and bicycle traffic in each direction and wide sidewalks of linear public space. Planting and surface design slow traffic, while new spaces for shops and restaurants engage occupants of the bridge. The architecture of the bridge provides structure and creates spaces that support train, bicycle and pedestrian transit. Wide sidewalks and shaded plazas punctuate areas of circulation and tie the design into the activity of the Downtown Mall on the north edge and the neighborhood

life of Belmont on the south. Views to Monticello and the Blue Ridge Mountains connect the experience of downtown Charlottesville with an awareness of the city's local and regional context. The inclines of the surface both refer to the Piedmont topography of mountains and valleys, and express the movement of the water on the surface as planted swales collect and treat run-off.

City X-ing will be a flexible space, closed to automobile traffic on weekend market days, or for events such as parades and festivals. The surface landscape can guide the development of additional park space along the rail tracks. Through a public-private partnership consisting of two phases, the bridge park and surrounding development can be a vibrant stage for movement and activity in the city of Charlottesville.

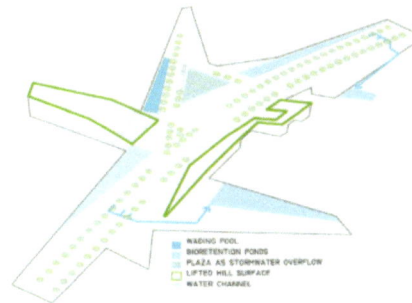

LANDSCAPE AND WATER STRATEGY:

WADING POOL
BIORETENTION PONDS
PLAZA AS STORMWATER OVERFLOW
LIFTED HILL SURFACE
WATER CHANNEL

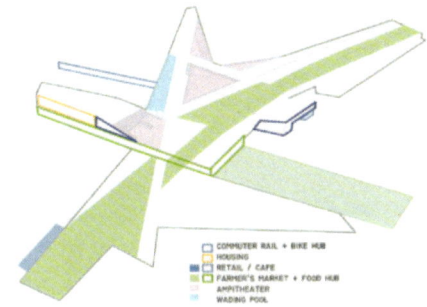

PROGRAM AND CIRCULATION

COMMUTER RAIL + BIKE HUB
HOUSING
RETAIL / CAFE
FARMER'S MARKET + FOOD HUB
AMPHITEATER
WADING POOL

ADVISOR: Shiqiao Li; TEAM: Kathleen Susan Lavelle, Benjamin Lawson, Katharine E Stabler, Emma Jane Wilkinson, Ravon Allen, Greg Benson, Nick Knodt, Lauren Shumate, Haojun Zhan, Rachel Stevens, Jack Cochran

THE LATENT VORTEX OF FLOW

The Belmont Bridge obscures a vortex in the urban fabric. The site is a significant hinge point between the mall and Belmont. The rebuilding of the bridge is understood as an opportunity to rebuild the urban fabric. This project proposes to abandon the idea of a bridge for vehicular traffic and, instead, free the space for all other means of movement and activities. Traffic can be effectively re-routed over adjacent existing bridges. The new building along the perimeter frames the space.

The objective of this proposal is about the subtraction of the constructed physical and built environment to allow for a vortex of activities and program. A railroad crossing at grade allows movement across the tracks except for at very few moments throughout the day when trains need to pass. A new pedestrian bridge allows for an alternative crossing at all times and views out into the larger region. The gained generous continuous public urban space is a new square for Belmont and allows for many activites that are not limited to consumption. The surface of the square provides gradients of paved and impervious areas to accomodate a variety of sports, play and occupation.

This space will encourage the further growth of residential and mixed-use areas in Belmont, integrating it with the Downtown Mall. Regrading the space to a valley-like condition will provide simple ways to manage stormwater and recharge the groundwater in a predominantly paved area.

left: after; below: before

ADVISOR: Jorg Sieweke; TEAM: Kate Adger Lemly, Anna Huizhong McMillen, Valeria Rivera Deneke, Victor Badami II, Minna Choi, Katherine Cullinan, Sarah E Schramm, Rebecca Hora, Luke Paskevich, Kirsten Ostberg

a PATH TO PEDESTRIAN BRIDGE

b PUBLIC PARK

c BIKE PATH CONNECTION TO GREENWAY

d PUBLIC PARK + WEEKLY FARMERS MARKET

e COMMUNITY FOOD INITIATIVE
COMMUNITY KITCHEN
FOOD PROCESSING CENTER
COMMUNITY GATHERING SPACE
AGRICULTURE + ENVIRONMENTAL RESOURCE CENTER
RAISED BED COMMUNITY GARDEN SPACE

f COMMUNITY ARTS INITIATIVE
STUDENT ART GALLERIES
AFTER-SCHOOL ARTS PROGRAM
STUDIO CO-OP CENTER
CRAFT CENTER

g RESIDENCES/ OFFICE SPACE

---- BIKE PATH

50 feet

EAST WATER STREET

4TH STREET SOUTHEAST

EAST SOUTH STREET

GARRETT STREET

GRAVES STREET

MONTICELLO

AVON STREET

With the existing traffic conditions, Belmont is currently cut off from downton.

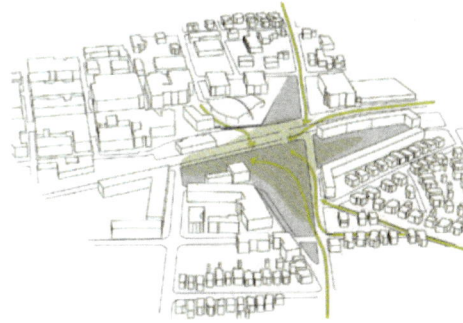

Regrading the topography allows for an intuitive and self-explanatory spatial cohesion.

The Vortex is defined by the activities and flows around and towards it.

The new building program along the perimeter frames the public space and consolidates blocks.

Relative to the wind direction, the space receives a fresh breeze in the summer heat island.

The scenographic geometry of the pedestrian bridge allows access at all times.

GAITWAY LOOP

Charlottesville's existing Belmont Bridge is the relic of an unnecessary bypass surgery, a monument to a missed opportunity that we hope to remedy with a less invasive procedure today. While the bridge does currently occupy the juncture between a pair of our town's most vital organs of residential, commercial and social activity, it fails to join them meaningfully. Our scheme aims to revive downtown Charlottesville by rejoining its most critical circulatory flows.

We propose the introduction of a new bridge, located east of the existing one. By reintroducing the connector's raised and ground-level lives with ramps and slopes friendly to vehicular, bicyclist and pedestrian traffic, we expect to activate a mediating zone between Belmont and the downtown mall. This diffuse lower-level territory, adjacent to Water Street, would serve as both destination and a catalyst for exercise and enterprise, encouraging the gradual cultivation of a productive landscape, more emblematic of Charlottesville's values.

Our proposal acknowledges the distinctiveness of the spheres it bridges, both physically and figuratively, by introducing a gradient of urban and more agrarian land use. We envision (1) new retail replacing the retaining wall currently dividing Water Street from the western terminus of the downtown mall, (2) an expanded and reconfigured music pavilion with occupiable canopy (3) a new farmer's market site, strategically planted with a public grove of fruit-bearing trees, and (4) an explicitly delineated loop of ground markings intended to help guide residents and tourists alike through a rejuvenated public space, dedicated to all of the best that Charlottesville has to offer.

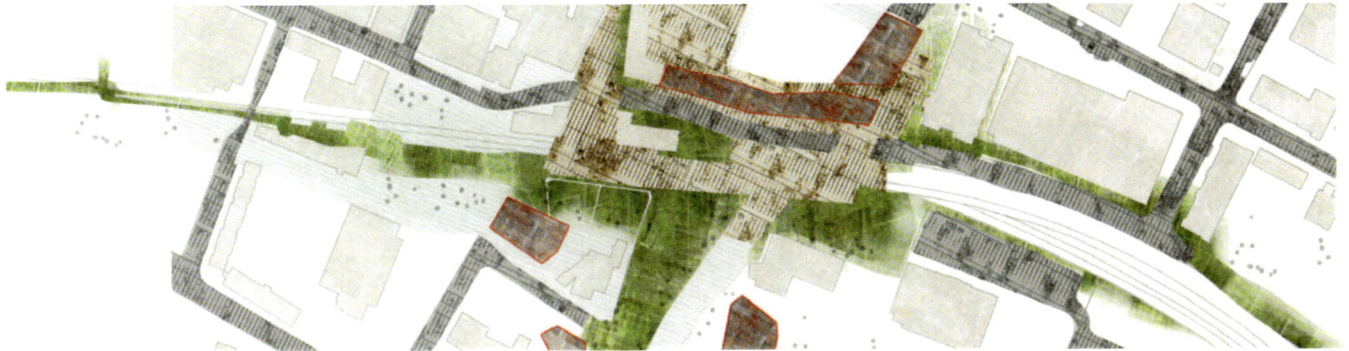

ADVISORS: John Quale, Sara Osborne; TEAM: Timothy John Morris, Stephanie Marie Smid, Kelsey Nicole Bixler, Timothy Edwards, Diana Fang, Hugo Fenaux, John Conroe Spiess, Andrew Brown, Megan Driscoll, Kate Boles, Justin Alstice

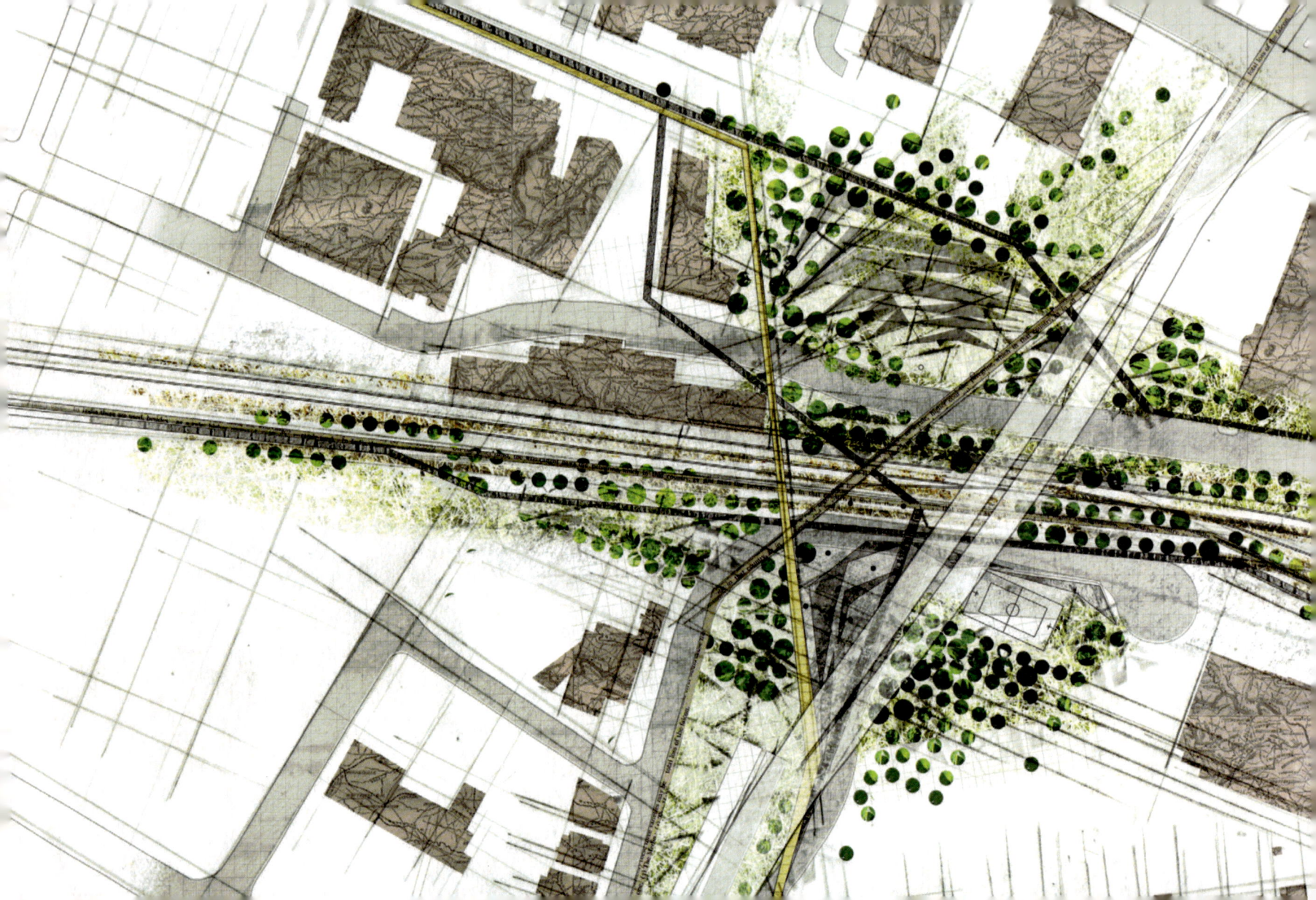

CIRCUS OF SPEEDS

The current Belmont Bridge spans across the site of the original Charlottesville Circus grounds—a space that once served as a hub of spectacle and activity. This site has been neutralized by a bridge that separates a city and a neighborhood, bypassing the once lively ground beneath the bridge in an effort to move more quickly through space. The Circus of Speeds seeks to remedy this disconnect by reclaiming the space below the Belmont Bridge and re-imagining it as a space of activity and movement that connects Belmont to the Downtown Mall through a network of paths for both cars and people. The new Belmont Bridge adopts a different form, allowing the Downtown Mall to extend into the space along the railroad tracks through a constructed amphitheater. Infrastructural ruins [columns, girders, beams] from the removed bridge serve as a reminder of the former structure and begin to shape spaces of activity—a skate park, a farmer's market, a graffiti wall and a hiking trail. Pedestrian paths weave through these spaces, connecting important nodes within the Downtown Mall and Belmont—the most notable of these paths is a raised bridge for bikers and pedestrians that links the main spaces of activity in both districts.

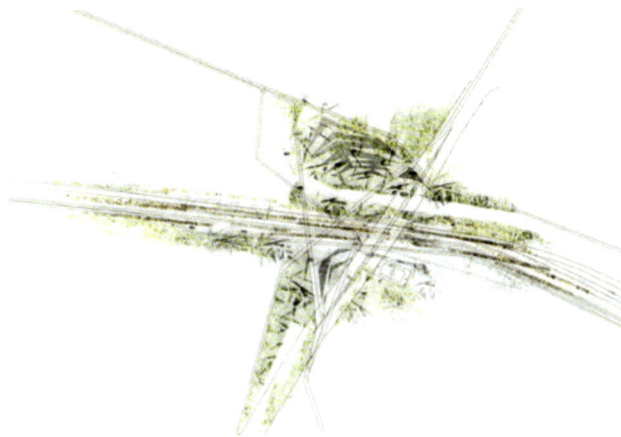

Ground Plane : triangulated surface

Canopy : speed registration

ADVISOR: Earl Mark; TEAM: Hayley Rachel Yeager, Julia Campbell Spong, Carrie Daiana Cardona, Henry John Hofmann, Mariam Rahmatullah, Gebremichael, Tamrat, Meagan McFadden, Polly Smith, Matthew Pinyan, Chelsea Dewitt, Emily Peterson

Two bridges intertwined; a path for cars and a path for people.

BELMONT

① BRIDGE | Cross Section

DOWNTOWN MALL

② AMPHITHEATER | Folded Groundplane

0   10   20   40 feet

WEST

③ UNDER THE BRIDGE | Belmont Skatepark & Market Space

0   10   20   40 feet

THE CONFLUENCE

During the original expansion of the railroad, Charlottesville was cleanly lacerated by a coal line. It has borne the scar handsomely ever since. The car eventually paved its way through the fabric of our city, and Charlottesville has continued to struggle with the steel-and-concrete connection that resulted between Downtown and Belmont. Now we see that the occlusion of natural human movement by these modes of transportation has reached a crossroads. These patterns demonstrate what many already know: a continuation of the urban fabric relies on reintegration of infrastructure with the pedestrian realm. Charlottesville's future will discover the organic patterns possible within the cultural folds of the city. The Confluence goes beyond reintegration.

The Confluence is not a bridge--at least, not by any conservative definition. It is not a one-dimensional corridor connecting two points like its predecessor. The Confluence is the entire depth and breadth of the volume in between. Its dimensions encompass the space, culture, history, future, and livelihood of the travelers between these two sides of the city - all making their existence known on this new palimpsest landscape.

Our "bridge" is an elevated urban park, a place of pause and a place of passing – across, through, over, under and around. It contains vertical nodes of commerce. It is also a cultural tapestry, stretched across an industrial chassis, creating an extension of the Downtown Pedestrian Mall with the character and scale of the Belmont neighborhood. It is a scaffold for farmer's markets, street performances, pick-up basketball games, New Year's fireworks, and Memorial Day picnics. In planning for the future, the best solution is often that which constrains the least, and only provides a fertile environment in which the future will grow as it may. The Confluence is a seed of the future.

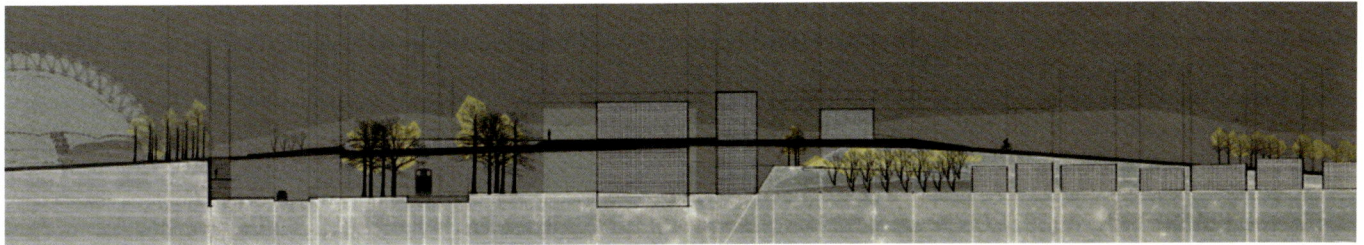

ADVISOR: Erin Hannegan; TEAM: Robert Jackson Bewley, Dirk Matthew Wilkins, Claire Venable Lester, Monique Morales, Kelvin Rafael Grullon, Hoa Nguyen, Derin Ozler, Will Green, Molly Baum, Katie Orr, Leah Erickson

East-West section (Downtown to Belmont)

VORTEX CORTEX CONTEXT

Between 1960 and 1975, the urban fabric of Charlottesville was dramatically altered and the character of the city's downtown changed in an enormous way. A program of urban renewal treated the area bounded by Ridge Street, 9th Street, Monticello and Market Street as a tabula rasa as the city's existing urban fabric was disturbed or destroyed to make way for a public housing development, a widened road and highway bridge designed to bypass the downtown, and parking facilities for a new pedestrian mall. The redevelopment of the Belmont Bridge presents the city with an opportunity to reflect upon both the positive and the negative impacts that modernist urban development had upon the city, and to adopt new modes of engagement with the city's historic fabric. Our project focuses upon the reactivation of the area bounded by these three projects with the goal of establishing fine-grained connections through the disconnected triangle between the mall, Belmont, and Garrett Street. In lieu of a single iconic bridge, we propose the construction of multiple passages over under and on the railroad tracks and the adaptive reuse of the post-industrial landscape located under the present bridge. The newly developed bridge territory will address the fragmentation of Charlottesville's downtown, while celebrating the success of the city's pedestrian mall and providing opportunities for economic growth on the other side of the tracks.

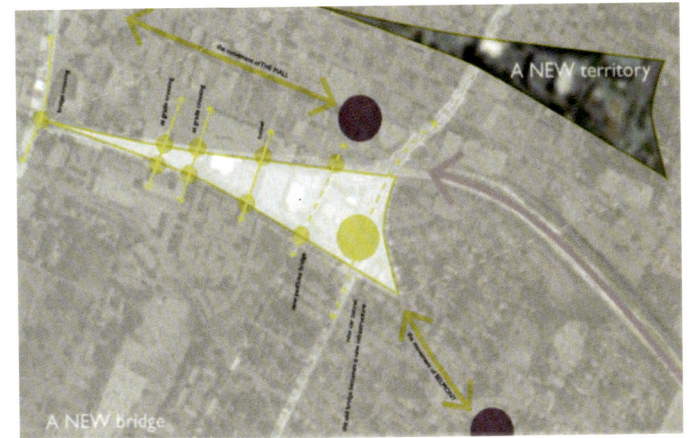

ADVISOR: Camille Behnke, Richard Guy Wilson; TEAM: Graham Harris Lohr, Olivia Christine Morgan, Carter Elizabeth Tata, Ashton Williams, Adam Poliner, Patton Roark, Catherine Nguyen, Hongfat Wu, David Mullen, Isaac Cohen, Annelise Pitts

THE BELMONT RIDGE

The nTelos Pavilion, completed in 2007, was envisioned as a bold punctuation mark to the downtown mall. As punctuation, it succeeds. As a monument to civic life, it does not. This proposal re-envisions the space of the pavilion and the adjacent area south of the mall as a multi-modal public space that extends rather than ends the mall, creating a physical and metaphorical connection to the people and the places of Belmont and beyond.

Our strategy reduces the four lanes of traffic on the bridge to two lanes and reallocates the remaining space to a pedestrian land bridge. Further, the bridge's span is reduced to 200 feet from 600, the minimum width necessary to span the train tracks. This is achieved by returning the earth that was removed to create the bowl of the pavilion. The effect is to diminish the visual impact of the bridge and reclaim the adjacent spaces on north and south sides of the train tracks for pedestrian use.

In the space formerly occupied by the pavilion, a mix of hardscape - including rubble recovered from the existing bridge - and planted form provides biofiltration and retention to address Charlottesville's looming water crisis while providing varied and fun surfaces for people of all ages. The greywater recovered in this zone can be used to irrigate the land bridge that spans the railroad tracks adjacent to the new, two-lane automobile crossing. The earthwork leads pedestrians to a downtown, multi-use park space. The site will provide a much needed area for Charlottesville's farmer's marker, host a band-shell for open-air concerts at night, and function as a public park in the intervening periods.

Belmont was Charlottesville's fastest growing neighborhood in 2010[1]

[1] Charlottesville City: Census 2010. http://www.coopercenter.org/demographics/virginia-population-estimates

In 2010, 27% of Charlottesville's population lived in either the Belmont or Venable neighborhoods

25% fewer people own cars in Belmont as compared with greater Charlottesville[2]

[2] City Data. http://www.coopercenter.org/demographics/virginia-population-estimates

Nearly a quarter of Belmont residents walk or bike to work[3]

[3] Ibid.

ADVISOR: Michael Petrus; TEAM: Kathryn Elizabeth Fowler, Eric Michael Gillwald, Aliaa Abdel Hamid Sabry, Morgan Taylor Stackman, Aneesha Baharani, Andrea Brennan, Rachel Vassar, Parker Sutton, Jonathan Bernard, Isaac Hametz

MUDDY HANDS

IÑAKI ALDAY, ELWOOD R. QUESADA PROFESSOR OF ARCHITECTURE AND CHAIR OF THE
DEPARTMENT OF ARCHITECTURE, UNIVERSITY OF VIRGINIA

Se le vio, caminando entre fusiles,
por una calle larga,
salir al campo frío,
aún con estrellas, de la madrugada.
Mataron a Federico
cuando la luz asomaba.
El pelotón de verdugos
No osó mirarle la cara.
Todos cerraron los ojos;
rezaron: ¡ni Dios te salva!
Muerto cayó Federico
—sangre en la frente y plomo en las entrañas—.
…Que fue en Granada el crimen
sabed —¡pobre Granada!—, en su Granada…

Antonio Machado, "El Crimen fue en Granada"
1936, en "Poesías de la Guerra", 1938

He was seen walking between rifles
down a long street,
coming upon the cold field
which still stars at early dawn.
They killed Federico
when daylight appeared.
The squad of executioners
dared not to look at his face.
All had shut their eyes.
They prayed: Not even God can save you!
Dead fell Federico-
blood on his forehead and lead in his entrails.
…Oh, that the crime was in Granada.
Let all know it! Poor Granada! In his Granada!

Antonio Machado, "The Crime Occurred in Granada"
1938, in "Poetry of the War Years", 1938

Translation by Willis Barnstone, "The Dream Below the Sun", 1981

Antonio Machado's poem "The Crime Ocurred in Granada" is about the murder of the Spanish poet Federico García Lorca on August 19, 1936. Lorca, a socially committed writer, was killed at the onset of the Spanish Civil War (1936-1937) by the forces of the future dictator, Francisco Franco. The poem was first published in memory of Lorca in the newspaper Ayuda on October 17, 1936.

Machado was one of the most outstanding Spanish poets of the "Generation of '98". After a first period of introspective poetry, he commits socially, as Federico Garcia Lorca or Miguel Hernandez, with the reality of his country, the women of Castilla and the existence of the so-called "two Spain". His initial poetry, intimate and sensorial, was closely related to the French aesthetes of the fin de siècle as Verlaine. The Spanish landscape is part of an indulgent yet beautiful gaze, intertwined with memories and dreams. Years later, with the publication of "Campos de Castilla" (Castilian Countryside) in 1912, the lyric beauty of the places and their inhabitants imbibes a conscious look about the life, the culture and the emotions of the people of his environment. His poetry exposes, analyzes and judges the socio-economic conditions of the country.

The poet kept throughout all his life a teaching activity as Professor of French in several high schools, a way to give back the education he received in the paradigmatic "Institución Libre de Enseñanza" (Free Institution of Learning). This institution educated most of the generation of intellectuals and politicians who tried the democratic experience of the Second Republic. The newborn democracy ended tragically after three years of civil war, under the eyes of the whole world and as the prologue to the World War II. Machado died exiled in France in 1939, before the end of the Spanish war.

Eight years later, two after the end of the apocalyptic world war, Magnum Photos was founded. Robert Capa and Henri Cartier-Bresson, along with Rodger and "Chim" Seymour, survivors of the war, created the cooperative to reflect their independent natures as both people and photographers, reporters and artists at the same time. Cartier-Bresson explains: "With Magnum was born the necessity for telling a story. Capa said to me: 'Don't keep the label of a surrealist photographer. Be a photojournalist. If not you will fall into mannerism. Keep surrealism in your little heart, my dear. Don't fidget. Get moving!'" Capa and Chim, two of the four founders, died in a decade while covering other wars. Years later, in 1979, the Brazilian Sebastiao Salgado joined Magnum until 1994.

While in Magnum and after establishing his own agency, Amazonas Images, Salgado has edited these books: Other Americas (1986), An Uncertain Grace (1990), Workers (1993), Terra (1997), Migrations (2000), The Children: Refugees and Migrants (2000), The End of Polio

Previous page: Iñaki Alday, Quesada Professor and Chair, Department of Architecture meets with students to discuss their proposals. [Photos Courtesy: Wimer]

Margarita Jover Biboum, Department of Architecture Lecturer, meets with students to discuss proposals. Photo Courtesy: Wimer]

(2003), The Cradle of Inequity (2005), Sahel: The End of the Road (2004), Africa (2007). There is no innocence in any single title; there is no shot without bullet. His eyes have brought to our eyes the conditions of life and work of different social and ethnic groups around the world through his extraordinary, yet terrifying, pictures of human landscapes.

Beauty, yes! Sublime beauty in each image. All of them are black and white images, always with human presence at different scales. From the portraits of "Children", with young kids from Latin America, Africa, Asia and Europe, to desolate or exuberant landscapes in which the human figure is embedded until being part of the lights and shadows of the place. In "Migrations", a tiny, almost cartoonish inverted "Y" shape figure, tries to escape form the patrol in the infinite landscape of the border between Mexico and the United States. The words of Cartier-Bresson are still valid; each image is expressing the necessity of explaining a story. There is no surplus of images, as there is no story without the need to be told. And all of them take the breath of the observer, sometimes striking painfully, sometimes questioning quietly.

The Spanish philosopher Jose Ortega y Gasset, in his book of 1924 "La deshumanizacion del Arte" (The Dehumanization of the Art), develops the Kant's concept of 'aesthetic pleasure and the distinction between 'aesthetic judgment' and 'moral judgment'. The art gets rid of the human identification to be judged only aesthetically: "the artistic object is